Perfect*

To Don,
It's a pleasure to meet you,
and I pray that God blesses
you through these pages.

In Christ's love,
David Rex Gosnell
Tampa Fl . July 13 2013

It's all for God's perfect glory!

Perfect*

What Jesus Teaches Us about
Building Intimacy with God

DAVID REX GOSNELL

CROSSBOOKS

CrossBooks™
A Division of LifeWay
1663 Liberty Drive
Bloomington, IN 47403
www.crossbooks.com
Phone: 1-866-879-0502

First published by CrossBooks 3/7/2013

ISBN: 978-1-4627-2550-2 (sc)
ISBN: 978-1-4627-2552-6 (hc)
ISBN: 978-1-4627-2551-9 (e)

Library of Congress Control Number: 2013903407

Printed in the United States of America

This book is printed on acid-free paper.

To Bob and Shirley Christie

Contents

Acknowledgments

I express my deepest gratitude to those who have encouraged and supported me in my Christian walk and ministry through the years. You have made this book possible.

- » My heavenly Father: thank you for loving me so much that you adopted me as your child and for guiding me to write this book. You get the credit for everything of value.

- » Mary Gosnell, Gary Regoli, Bob and Shirley Christie, and Sandra Hoggard: thank you for reading various drafts of this book. Each of you provided valuable insight that made it so much better.

- » Bob and Shirley Christie: thank you for your friendship, guidance, mentoring, support, encouragement and, most of all, your prayers.

- » Gene and Debbie Bodden, Doug and Rachelle Hutchens, Richard and Mary Kalil, Frank and Tricia Wollett: thank you for many years of close friendship.

- » The wonderful, selfless people of New Hope Community Church in Dunedin, Florida: thank you for your support, patience, and encouragement during five years of ministry together.

» W. L. Baker, Ralph Harris, Courtney Wilson, Dan Shaddock, Randy Hyde, Gary Gates, Mike Rogers, Rick Pendleton, and Andy Strachan, my pastors over the years: thank you so much for faithfully proclaiming God's message in word and deed.

» Herbert Gabhart, Roy Helton, John Tulloch, and Robert Byrd, my Bible professors and mentors at Belmont College: thank you for inspiring me to seek deeper understanding of God's word.

» All those who endured my teaching in various Sunday school and Bible study classes over forty years: thank you for your participation and patience. I'm sure I learned more than you did.

» Viola Davis and Carl Zenkert, fellow teachers who are now with the Lord: thank you for your wisdom and the grace to impart it.

» My parents, Paul Rex and Mary Frances Gosnell, who are also with the Lord: thank you for your perfect example of Christian parents and for keeping me on an upward path.

» Our children, Sandra, Jennifer, Andrew, and Jonathan: thank you for your love and for enduring an imperfect but sincere father.

» My wife Mary: thank you for your abiding love, understanding, and patience. I love you more than life itself.

INTRODUCTION

INTIMACY WITH GOD

*I am in them and You are in Me. May they be made
completely one, so the world may know You have sent
Me and have loved them as You have loved Me.*
—John 17:23

One of my favorite ways to spend time in college was in late-night discussions with friends. Usually we gathered in someone's dorm room or apartment. The range of topics was truly breathtaking. Women and sports topped the list, of course, but we also delved into cars, politics, technology, exercise, and future modes of transportation (jet packs, you know). As young male engineering students, we clearly knew more than just about anyone else alive, and we brought our vast intellect and understanding to bear on almost any issue or problem you could imagine.

One of the most entertaining topics was "the most important thing in the world." Each guy tried to one-up everyone else by explaining, in great detail, why his particular area of interest was the most important one of all. Energy was my favorite. For one of my friends it was national politics. And one guy never thought about anything but the current college football standings.

Occasionally someone would say the most important thing in the world is interpersonal relationships, but as a group we probably knew less about that than anything else.

One time we were on this topic and someone used the word "intimacy." I had heard the phrases "intimate apparel" and "intimate with a woman," but I had no actual experience with either. Based on the comments that followed, it was clear that I wasn't alone in my ignorance. My friends and I were at a loss to understand the true concept of intimacy. No one seemed to be familiar with mutual self-giving. Unconditional commitment never crossed our minds. And the idea of sharing personal thoughts or feelings caused fear and panic. Needless to say, the intimacy discussion didn't last long.

Looking back with a little more experience and perspective, the meaning and value of intimacy are much clearer. Building intimacy with my wife, Mary, continues to be one of life's most wonderful experiences.

Most of us have experienced an intimate relationship with a parent, sibling, spouse, or friend, but that's not true for everyone. Some seek intimacy for a lifetime but never experience it. Others never make intimacy a priority and settle for relationships that fail to reach their potential. Some people don't even realize they are missing it.

Intimacy requires love, commitment, and communication. It's based on sharing life together. A genuinely intimate relationship with another human being is both fulfilling and valuable and can be one of life's greatest joys.

But have you ever wondered what an intimate relationship with God would be like? To talk with the Creator face to face? To be one in mind and heart with the Almighty? To share love, commitment, and communication with their inventor?

Before Adam and Eve sinned, they had that kind of relationship with God in the garden of Eden. Can you imagine what it was like to walk with God "in the cool of the day" (Genesis 3:8 KJV)?

That's not the kind of intimacy most people normally experience, but it does happen. In the Bible, the people who had the greatest impact on their generation were the ones who were the most intimate with God. Abraham talked directly with God, even bargaining with Him over Sodom and Gomorrah (see Genesis 18). Moses was so intimate with God that "the Lord spoke with Moses face to face, just as a man speaks with his friend" (Exodus 33:11). And David was so close to the Lord that Samuel called him "a man after his own heart" (1 Samuel 13:14 KJV).

Our ultimate example of intimacy with God is Jesus of Nazareth. He was called "the Son of David" (Matthew 1:1, 12:23, 21:9) for more than one reason. First, He was David's direct descendant (see Matthew 1:6–16). He was also the ultimate fulfillment of the promise that God had made to David that "I will raise up after you your descendant, who is one of your own sons, and I will establish his kingdom ... and his throne will be established forever" (1 Chronicles 17:11,14).

And Jesus was, even more than David, a man after God's own heart. He thought like His Father. He behaved like His Father. He desired, more than anything, to do His Father's will. God said of Him, "This is My beloved Son. I take delight in Him. Listen to Him!" (Matthew 17:5). Jesus pointed out to the Jews that "the Father and I are one" (John 10:30).

Jesus expanded on this intimacy with His disciples in the upper room: "Believe Me that I am in the Father and the Father is in Me ... Because I live, you will live too. In that day you will know that I am in My Father, you are in Me, and I am in you. The one who has My commands and keeps them is the one who loves Me. And the one who loves Me will be loved by My Father. I also will love him and will reveal Myself to him" (John 14:11,19–21).

Jesus emphasized intimacy with God in various ways throughout His time on earth:

> » He appointed twelve apostles "to be with Him" (Mark 3:14). It took three years of daily walking with Jesus for them to learn enough to fulfill His purpose for their lives.

> » In the parable of the prodigal son, the older brother refused to welcome his brother home. But his father implored, "Son, you are always with me, and everything I have is yours" (Luke 15:31). The father wanted to experience intimacy with both of his sons.

> » Jesus said that when the king separates the sheep from the goats at the end of time, those who lack a relationship with God will hear the fateful words, "Depart from me, you who are cursed" (Matthew 25:41). Separation from God, the total absence of intimacy, will be the ultimate punishment.

> » On the other hand, He told His apostles in the upper room, "In My Father's house are many dwelling places … I will come back and receive you to Myself, so that where I am you may be also" (John 14:2–3). Close, intimate fellowship with God will be the ultimate reward.

> » When Jesus prayed for all believers just before He was betrayed, He asked for intimacy for all of us: "May they all be one, as You, Father, are in Me and I am in You. May they also be one in Us, so the world may believe You sent Me … I am in them and You are in Me. May they be made completely one, so the world may know You have sent Me and have loved them as You have loved Me" (John 17:21,23).

Look again at John 14:20. Jesus said this intimacy would be so great that

He would be *in* you and you *in* Him. How that works is a mystery, but the gospel writers continued the theme: "God wanted to make known to those among the Gentiles the glorious wealth of this mystery, which is Christ in you, the hope of glory" (Colossians 1:27). "This is how we know that we remain in Him and He in us: He has given to us from His Spirit … And we have come to know and to believe the love that God has for us. God is love, and the one who remains in love remains in God, and God remains in him (1 John 4:13,16).

Clearly, an intimate relationship with God was of primary importance to Jesus and His followers. Perhaps the best way for us to understand this intimacy is to draw an analogy with the marriage relationship. When God created marriage He declared, "This is why a man leaves his father and mother and bonds with his wife, and they become one flesh" (Genesis 2:24). More than just a physical union, God designed marriage to be a relationship in which the man and woman become one in all other areas as well. Dr. Gary Chapman has described that intimacy in this way:

> The Hebrew word for *one* is the same Hebrew word used in Deuteronomy 6:4: "Hear, O Israel: the Lord our God, the Lord is one." This word speaks of a unity made up of distinct parts. In the case of God, it is three who are one—Father, Son, and Holy Spirit—one God. In marriage, it is two who are to become one. Such oneness is at the heart of what marriage is all about. *Oneness* is a synonym for *intimacy* … God designed marriage to be the most intimate of all human relationships. We are going to share life—intellectually, socially, emotionally, spiritually, and physically—and we are going to share life to such a degree that it can be said of us, we become *one*.[1]

---

1   Gary D. Chapman, *Covenant Marriage* (Nashville: B&H Publishing Group, 2003), 34-35.

Similarly, God wants us to have an intimate relationship with Him, to be one with Him. Just as Jesus was one with His Father, God wants us to be one with Him. This oneness isn't just an artifact of biblical times; He desires intimacy with every one of His children. And again, just as in the Bible, God works best through the people who are closest to—that is, most intimate with—Him.

The main goal of this book is to help you establish and develop an intimate relationship with God. Notice again what Jesus said to His disciples about the one who loves Him: "I also will love him and will reveal Myself to him" (John 14:21). We see that this kind of intimacy is based on love and self-revelation. God loves you, and He wants you to love Him. He also reveals Himself to you, and He wants you to reveal yourself to Him.

Love always seeks the greatest good. True love cares deeply for the one who is loved, and love begets the kind of commitment that enables the relationship to endure. God is the very embodiment of love, and His greatest command is for you to love Him in return. Love is crucial.

Mutual self-revelation means that the two people disclose their thoughts and feelings. They tell each other their secrets without holding anything back. When you reveal yourself to another person, you trust that they won't betray you. More than a few people have shared their feelings with another, only to be hurt when those feelings were made public.

God, on the other hand, always treats our feelings with care and respect. Although He already knows all about you, God wants you to tell Him your needs and desires, admit your shortcomings and failures, and disclose your true thoughts and feelings. In turn, He wants you to come to know and understand Him as fully as possible.

God reveals Himself, His love, and His commitment to us in various ways: through nature, the Bible, Christian teaching and preaching, and our circumstances. He also communicates with us through prayer.

In fact, prayer can be defined simply as communication with God. Not only do we hear God speak to us through prayer, but we can also disclose ourselves to Him. To build an intimate relationship with God, it is vital that you share your thoughts and feelings with Him, and you can do that through prayer.

So in this book we will investigate what Jesus teaches us about building intimacy with God through prayer. After all, Jesus spent considerable time praying. He was in constant contact with His Father. If anyone knows how to approach prayer, it's Jesus. He taught His disciples, in word and deed, everything they needed to know about prayer—and He can teach us, too.

This book examines the Model Prayer in detail because it was Jesus' response when one of His disciples asked Him, "Lord, teach us to pray" (Luke 11:1). These men had observed Jesus praying, and they knew that He frequently got up before the sun to pray by Himself. They had seen Him pray before feeding five thousand people, and they knew that He "often withdrew to deserted places and prayed" (Luke 5:16).

Through all of these episodes, Jesus' disciples came to realize there was a direct connection between His prayers and His power. They may not have fully understood it at the time, but because prayer is so essential to our relationship with God, they were actually asking for the keys to building intimacy in that relationship, and that is what Jesus gave them.

The prayer Jesus spoke is one of the shortest and simplest prayers recorded in the Bible yet is arguably the most profound. It can be said in half a minute, but it is the key to all the important aspects of our relationship with God.

As documented in Matthew 6:9–13 as part of the Sermon on the Mount, the Model Prayer consists of nine simple phrases:

Our Father in heaven,
Your name be honored as holy.
Your kingdom come.
Your will be done on earth as it is in heaven.
Give us today our daily bread.
And forgive us our debts, as we also have forgiven our debtors.
And do not bring us into temptation,
but deliver us from the evil one.
For Yours is the kingdom and the power and the glory forever.
Amen.

The first phrase is the salutation. The next three focus on God and involve some action on our part. The next four are petitions we make to God. The final phrase is a doxology of praise.

We will examine each of these phrases in detail as we seek to understand just how Jesus exhorted us to approach our heavenly Father in prayer. What we will find, without question, is God's kingdom, power, and glory.

In addition, we will discover what Jesus has to teach us about prayer that truly communicates with God. And we will see how this kind of prayer nourishes an intimate and enduring relationship with our heavenly Father.

Part One

Coming to God in Prayer

God is more important than I am. For most of us, that's a bitter pill to swallow. In my world, I really want to be the most important person. I want to be at the top of my totem pole. Numero uno. Da man. Why shouldn't the world revolve around me?

The truth is, however, I don't live in my world. I live in God's world. He created it and sustains it, so He owns it. It's His totem pole, and He's at the top. Da man and da God.

What does that mean to me? One thing it means is that even though I would like to set the agenda when communicating with God, I don't get to do that. God sets the agenda, purpose, approach, and everything else. He's got the power. He's got the authority. I may as well get used to it. In a relationship with God, He's always the senior partner, so I must come to Him on His terms.

That's not as bad as it may sound because God has a love for me that knows no limits. He always has my best interests at heart. What God wants for me is better than even my own egocentric desires. What He offers is superior to anything I can imagine. The prayer agenda that God has set is already the best one possible. I should want to get used to it.

So it's time to come to God in prayer. In its purest form, prayer is simply a conversation with God that is based on a relationship with

Him. Thought of in these terms, prayer is similar in many respects to a conversation with another human being with whom we have a relationship. The relationship forms the foundation for the conversation. The stronger and more intimate the relationship, the better and more fulfilling the conversation. Let's see how that relationship and that conversation get started.

1

PERFECT? REALLY?

Be perfect, therefore, as your heavenly Father is perfect.
—Matthew 5:48

YEARS AGO, I ATTENDED A seminar about effective communication. The speaker said that when most people are asked "How are you?" they simply reply "Fine, how are you?" He pointed out that the question is not really a question but a greeting, and that the default "fine" is simply recognition of the greeting. "To really stand out," he continued, "you should use a unique comeback to show that you are unique. Say something like 'great,' 'superfine,' or 'outstanding' and say it with conviction and excitement! Then people will pay attention and want to know all about you."

This idea seemed a little over the top to me, but I decided to try it. After all, who doesn't want to be seen as unique? It took some time before I was comfortable replying "great," especially since I didn't always feel so great, but I began to get results. The other person would usually give me a strange look, apparently wondering what was so great about me. Although I was disappointed that it wasn't obvious, I kept it up because I felt clever for using such a unique greeting.

It wasn't long, however, before I realized that other people were also great. It seemed that I wasn't so clever after all. I decided that I had to look for a new, even more unique greeting, and after some experimentation, I settled on "perfect!" This response usually prompted some skepticism, which suited me just fine. I knew that I couldn't prove that I was, in fact, perfect, but I was drawing interesting responses. "Perfect? Really?" said one man. "That must take a lot of work!"

Time went on, and one day I heard a coworker use the phrase "perfect in every conceivable fashion" when talking (more than a little sarcastically) about some work that had been done by another group. *What a bizarre expression*, I thought. Pretty much nothing is perfect in every conceivable fashion, so if anything actually was, it would have to be totally unique! This was definitely the phrase I had been looking for.

Now when someone asks how I am and hears the reply "perfect in every conceivable fashion," he or she is put on notice that I am completely unique and not to be trifled with. People who hear it for the first time are usually somewhat bemused. They'll comment on the obvious impossibility, whether I'm really hitting on all eight cylinders, or how their meager "fine" pales in comparison. Most of my friends just smile, sigh, and roll their eyes. Whatever the response, I know that I've at least caused someone to think.

Okay, I'll admit the obvious. I fully acknowledge that I am as far from perfect as anyone else. I've caused just as many problems, hurt just as many people, and behaved just as selfishly as most other people I know. I make mistakes every day just like everyone else. So I have to admit that I'm not perfect after all. But it's still fun to say it.

I'm sure you'd agree there's no such thing as the perfect person. Human existence is too difficult, complex, and frustrating to even come close to perfection. None of us can claim to be perfect. We would consider anyone who did to be either a bold liar, a facetious clown, or certifiably insane. (Um, I think I'll go with the second one.)

Jesus Is the Exception

Enter Jesus, the one single Exception, the only perfect man who ever lived. How can we say that? The Bible clearly shows that Jesus is God Himself, the God who truly is perfect in every conceivable fashion.

How do we know that God is perfect? Here are a few ways.

God is infinite because He created everything that exists.

The first statement in the Bible is "in the beginning God created the heavens and the earth" (Genesis 1:1). He literally spoke the universe into existence; only a being with infinite power could do that.

The universe is an interesting place. Though scientists hold differing theories about its structure, and thus varying estimates of its size, the general consensus is that the universe is at least ten billion light-years across. A light-year is the distance light travels in a year, which is almost six trillion miles. That's a 6 with twelve zeros behind it. That distance alone is difficult for us to conceive. Multiply that by ten billion, and we've added ten more zeros.

One time I ran a half-marathon (that's 13.1 miles) and it seemed so long that I almost quit before the finish. I live approximately seven hundred miles from where I was born. They tell us that the moon is about 240,000 miles from earth, which is ninety-three million miles from the sun. I can make sense of those distances, although that last one is a stretch. But 60,000,000,000,000,000,000,000 miles? I don't know about you, but I have no way of even comprehending that distance. Add to that the likelihood that the universe is expanding, and you have to conclude that what God created is truly of unimaginable size.

And what's out there? Recent photos from the Hubble Space Telescope show that many stars we see are actually galaxies, or even clusters of galaxies. Scientists now think that billions of galaxies exist, each containing at least millions of stars. That means that there are at least one quadrillion stars in the universe (that's right—fifteen zeros). Our sun is a star, and it's thousands of times bigger than the earth.

There are a lot of really big objects in a really vast space. Psalm 147:4

says that God "counts the number of the stars; He gives names to all of them." So not only did God make all of those stars, He remembers their names as well!

One could examine many other aspects of the world around us, such as the astonishingly large number of particles in just a drop of pond water, not to mention the many life forms in that same drop. Instead, since this isn't really a science book, I'll stop here and restate the point: it took someone with infinite intellect and power to create our incredible universe *simply by speaking it into existence.* That someone, of course, is God; God is infinite.

"Our Lord is great, vast in power; His understanding is infinite" (Psalm 147:5).

God is holy.

In the Bible, the word "holy" carries the meaning "set apart." No one is set apart in the way that God is, but a human analogy would be a sports star at the top of his game or a musical performer who sells the most records and attracts the biggest concert crowds. Because of their outstanding accomplishments, and especially when these stars use their fame to help people by doing good works, they are revered by their followers.

This is a similar idea to revering God. He can do things that we can't do, and He's perfectly righteous, so He is to be revered above all else. The world may revere sport stars and rock stars as set apart from the rest of us, but God is the one who is really holy.

To say that God is holy means that He is other than us, completely different from us. Being infinite, God has no beginning and no end. Along with space, He created time, so He is not bound by either. We are finite beings with finite beginnings in time and finite life spans on earth. Since God created us, He is above us in all aspects, separate from us. We cannot sense Him with our eyes or ears or in any other physical way. The only things we can know about Him are what He reveals to us. God is holy.

God has no weaknesses, errors, or problems.

You will never find anything that God has done wrong. He makes no mistakes, and the Bible confirms it: "The Rock—His work is perfect; all His ways are entirely just. A faithful God, without prejudice, He is righteous and true" (Deuteronomy 32:4). "God—His way is perfect; the word of the Lord is pure. He is a shield to all who take refuge in Him" (2 Samuel 22:31).

Being infinite in power, infinite in knowledge, and completely holy, God is simply perfect.

The Model of Perfection

Now, back to Jesus. The Bible makes the seemingly outlandish claim that this Jewish man who lived two millennia ago is actually God. Some people want to dispute that claim. How do we know it's true?

The evidence shows that Jesus has God's power.

Taken together, the evidence is overwhelming:

» Jesus was born by a virgin, showing His holy nature.

» He walked on water and calmed a raging storm at sea, showing His power over nature.

» He healed many people who were blind, lame, or leprous, showing His power over illness and disease.

» He cast out demons, showing His power over spiritual forces.

» He brought at least three people back to life and then rose from the dead Himself, showing His power over life and death.

» Many aspects of Jesus' birth, life, death, and resurrection were predicted hundreds of years in advance by God's prophets.

Consult the recommended reading in the appendix if you want more details. The truth is that Jesus came to earth and lived as a man, died, rose again, and ascended to heaven. Only God could do that.

The Bible says that Jesus is God.

John began his gospel by speaking about Jesus: "In the beginning was the Word, and the Word was with God, and the Word was God. He was with God in the beginning. All things were created through Him, and apart from Him not one thing was created that has been created" (John 1:1–3). The apostle Paul said that Jesus existed "in the form of God" (Philippians 2:6). Jesus Himself said, "The Father and I are one" (John 10:30). The Bible consistently testifies that Jesus is God in all aspects.

Jesus lived a perfect life.

The writers of the New Testament said it like this: "He made the One who did not know sin to be sin for us, so that we might become the righteousness of God in Him" (2 Corinthians 5:21). "For we do not have a high priest who is unable to sympathize with our weaknesses, but One who has been tested in every way as we are, yet without sin" (Hebrews 4:15). "You know that He was revealed so that He might take away sins, and there is no sin in Him" (1 John 3:5).

It wasn't easy for Jesus. He had to live through the same kind of turmoil, trials, and temptations that we experience plus a lot more. He was ridiculed, ostracized, jeered, beaten, and finally crucified. Yet through all of that He never reacted with poor judgment. He always responded with perfect love.

He taught the truth to those who were confused by life, no matter what their station. He spent time with the weak and lowly as well as the high and mighty. He helped women, children, soldiers, prostitutes, outcasts, and lepers. He patiently worked with those closest to Him, even though they consistently misunderstood His mission. He praised a destitute woman who gave what little money she had to God. He chastised the hypocritical religious leaders who appeared honorable while profiting from the weak and helpless. He preached to thousands and went out of His way to help one. Ultimately, He sacrificed His life for those He loved.

Throughout His whole life, Jesus showed us how to live. He gave us all the rules we need and always practiced what He preached. While exhorting us to serve, He served us. As He demanded total devotion, He devoted Himself totally. Through perfect love He encouraged us to love perfectly.

It's a simple argument. God is perfect. Since Jesus is God, Jesus is perfect. He demonstrated that by living a perfect life and showing us how to respond to life's challenges in a way that fully pleases God.

Our Turn

That brings us to the command that Jesus gave us just moments before He voiced the Model Prayer: "Be perfect, therefore, as your heavenly Father is perfect" (Matthew 5:48).

On the surface that seems a little excessive. We just agreed that no one is perfect but God Himself, and now Jesus comes along and tells us we have to be just as perfect as God? More than just a little excessive, it's impossible. Does He truly expect us to never lie, steal, cheat, dishonor God or our parents, or hurt anyone? To always love, help, and do the right thing, twenty-four hours a day, every single day of our lives? No, that's unachievable. After all, we're only human. So what can Jesus have in mind?

Must we be more mature?

Let's examine the word He uses. The Greek word translated "perfect" in this verse is *teleios*, which carries the idea of mature, complete, or perfect. It is usually translated "perfect" or "mature" in the New Testament. Here are two example verses:

» "However, among the mature (*teleios*) we do speak a wisdom, but not a wisdom of this age, or of the rulers of this age, who are coming to nothing" (1 Corinthians 2:6).

» "Brothers, don't be childish in your thinking, but be infants in evil and adult (*teleios*) in your thinking" (1 Corinthians 14:20).

So maybe Jesus isn't demanding utter perfection from us but maturity—spiritual maturity. He wants us to continue to strive to be as perfect as we can be. He knows that we are already marred by our own sin from the past, but He now commands that we move away from doing things our own way and become like Him in our thoughts, words, and actions.

We can check out this idea by examining what Jesus said leading up to this command. Remember He said, "Be perfect, therefore…" The word "therefore" means He's already given good reasons, so there must be some logic for us in the prior verses.

We'll find what we're seeking by looking back to verse 17 of this same chapter. Jesus was talking to large crowds of disciples from all parts of Israel. Many wanted to know if He was the Messiah who was predicted by God's prophets hundreds of years before. He had healed many of them, and now He told them about His true purpose in coming.

> Don't assume that I came to destroy the Law or the Prophets. I did not come to destroy but to fulfill. For I assure you: Until heaven and earth pass away, not the smallest letter or one stroke of a letter will pass from the law until all things are accomplished. Therefore, whoever breaks one of the least of these commandments and teaches people to do so will be called least in the kingdom of heaven. But whoever practices and teaches these commandments will be called great in the kingdom of heaven. For I tell you, unless your righteousness surpasses that of the scribes and Pharisees, you will never enter the kingdom of heaven. (Matthew 5:17–20)

Must we be better?

These verses make it clear that Jesus expects more from us than just obeying the letter of the law. After all, that's pretty much what the scribes and Pharisees did. They spent all their time making sure they fulfilled every single Jewish law. In fact, they continually added laws, many more than God Himself had commanded, so that it would appear they were the superhuman examples that every good Jew should aspire to be.

But while they fulfilled the letter of the law, they also frequently ignored its spirit. God's laws were in their minds but hadn't reached their hearts. Jesus pointed out their hypocritical ways and had no praise for their way of life. In fact, He told His listeners they had to be better than that just to enter God's kingdom. What a shock! The common people held their leaders in high esteem, so they were perplexed when Jesus said that anyone in God's kingdom has to be better.

Fortunately, Jesus clarified His point by giving several examples in Matthew 5:

> » In the Ten Commandments God prohibited murder. Jesus said to go beyond that to avoid even anger (21–26).

> » God also prohibited adultery in the Ten Commandments. Jesus said that if you lust after someone, you are already committing adultery in your heart, so you have to avoid lust too (27–30).

> » Jesus severely narrowed the allowable circumstances for divorce (31–32).

> » Jesus said that rather than making sure you just fulfill your oaths to God to avoid making any oaths at all (33–37).

> » Instead of taking justice and revenge into your own hands, Jesus commands you to turn the other cheek, go the extra mile, and lend to anyone who asks (38–42).

> » Finally, and most amazingly, Jesus said to go beyond loving your neighbor and hating your enemy. He commands that you love your enemies and pray for people who persecute you (43–47).

We see that Jesus sets a very high standard. The things He tells us to do don't come naturally. It takes real work to avoid anger, lust, and revenge and go around praying for people who are trying to hurt us.

Must we be like God?

A little thought makes it clear that Jesus is asking us to respond just like He does. Effectively, Jesus is telling us, "Since you want to be children of your heavenly Father, prove it by acting like Him. Like Father, like child." No wonder He said that our righteousness must surpass that of the scribes and Pharisees. They had no concept of what He was saying. Love your enemies? What kind of way to live is that?

But even if one could do all these things, is that really good enough? Remember, Jesus said to be perfect "as your heavenly Father is perfect" (Matthew 5:48). I'm pretty sure that no matter how hard I try, I'll never come close to God's level of perfection. And neither will you. Unless He has something else in mind, Jesus issued a command that we have absolutely no hope of obeying.

Perfect*!

Fortunately, there's one more way to interpret Jesus' command, and it depends on His efforts, not ours. He said these things about Himself:

> » "For God loved the world in this way: He gave His One and Only Son, so that everyone who believes in Him will not perish but have eternal life" (John 3:16).

> » "This is the work of God: that you believe in the One He has sent" (John 6:29).

> » "I have come that they may have life and have it in abundance" (John 10:10).

Paul said the purpose of his ministry was to "proclaim Him (Jesus), warning and teaching everyone with all wisdom, so that we may present everyone mature [*teleios*—perfect] in Christ" (Colossians 1:28). In Hebrews we see that Jesus, "after offering one sacrifice for sins forever, sat down at the right hand of God … For by one offering He has perfected forever those who are sanctified" (Hebrews 10:12,14).

These verses tell us that, although we can never be perfect on our own, Jesus will make us perfect if we simply believe in Him. What I cannot do, Jesus gladly does for me. By putting my faith in Him, the impossible can happen: God forgives all my sins, I become perfect in His eyes, and I experience abundant, eternal life. What an amazing turn of events!

Totally apart from my own efforts, I really am perfect. When God looks at me, He sees Jesus, the One who took my sins to the cross. Instead of my flaws, God sees the perfection of Christ. Jesus has paid the price for all my sins, so now I am, in fact, perfect—in every conceivable fashion. And it's true not just for me but for everyone who trusts in Jesus.

It's important to point out that this perfection comes with an asterisk, like this: perfect*. You've seen this before. When an athlete wins a competition or sets a record under some special condition, the record books will include a footnote. Perhaps a man runs the fastest marathon time ever, but it doesn't count for a world record because the course doesn't meet the international standards. Or a tennis player wins a match because her opponent retires due to an injury. That's what our perfection is like. We clearly aren't perfect on our own, but God, through His love, mercy, forgiveness and grace, has made us perfect*. Our perfection isn't inherent, it's inherited.

You truly can obey Jesus' command to be perfect, even as your heavenly Father is perfect. All your efforts are useless in this endeavor, but He has already provided the effort through His sacrifice on the cross. When you put your faith in Jesus, God makes you perfect*.

There really is a good reason for all this talk about being perfect*. We will see that our perfect God sits on a perfect throne in a perfect heaven. He is bathed in perfection; He is the source of it—which means that the imperfect is not allowed near.

But since we are now perfect* through Christ's sacrifice, we can approach God's perfect throne of grace. He has enabled us to have intimacy with Him, and that's where our prayer really begins.

CHAPTER SUMMARY

» As the infinite, holy Creator, God is perfect.

» Jesus, being God, is perfect in every conceivable fashion.

» Jesus lived a perfect life, showing us how we are to live.

» Jesus commands you to be perfect, even though you can't do that on your own.

» Jesus makes you perfect* by bringing you into a true, intimate relationship with God that is based on His love.

» Main point: God can make you perfect* through a relationship with Him.

Pursuing Perfect* Passion

For personal or group study

1. How perfect do you think you are? Have you ever tried to be perfect (or maybe just really good)? If so, what were the results of those efforts? Did you feel any closer to God?

2. How well do you feel that you understand God's perfection? Which of His perfect attributes (infinite, holy, just, pure, righteous, etc.) is the easiest for you to grasp? Which is most difficult?

3. Can you imagine what it was like for Jesus to live a perfect, sinless life, even though He experienced the same kinds of temptations that you have? Does His life inspire you to draw closer to God or does it discourage you from trying what seems to be impossible?

4. Hebrews 2:10, 5:9, and 7:28 state that Jesus was "perfected." If Jesus was already God, what does it mean that He was perfected?

5. Hebrews 10:14, 11:40, and 12:23 tell us that those of us who are saved through Christ have been made perfect. In what ways has God made you perfect*?

6. David sang in 2 Samuel 22:33 that "God is my strong refuge; He makes my way perfect." What do you think David meant by that?

7. Paul said in Philippians 3:10–11 that he wanted to know the "fellowship of His sufferings, being conformed to His death, assuming that I will somehow reach the resurrection from among the dead." Paul had already been beaten, imprisoned, stoned, and shipwrecked. Then he states in verse 12 that he was

not "already fully mature." Why would he need to experience more suffering to be complete? Can you think of ways that suffering could help make you more mature in Christ?

8. In Matthew 19:21 Jesus told the young man, "If you want to be perfect, go, sell your belongings and give to the poor, and you will have treasure in heaven. Then come, follow Me." How would selling his goods make the man perfect? Is there something about having lots of possessions that keeps a person from being a complete Christian? What changes, if any, do you feel you need to make based on this exchange between the young man and Jesus?

9. If you have never experienced God's mercy, grace, and forgiveness, what is keeping you from turning to Him by believing in Jesus' power to make you perfect*?

2

GOD: YOUR PERFECT FATHER

Our Father in heaven.
—Matthew 6:9

SUPPOSE YOU COULD SAY "MY father in the White House"; "my father, the chairman of General Motors,"; "my father, the owner of the New York Yankees"; or "my father, star of his own network TV show."

Think of the influence you'd have. What power, position, and prestige! Imagine the wealth and prosperity that you'd enjoy. To have a famous and powerful father—what an advantage in life!

Compare those with "Our Father in heaven." Now we're talking about "my Father, the creator of all that exists"; "my Father, the one with power over life and death"; "my Father, the sustainer of life"; or "my Father, the Savior of all who come to Him in faith."

How much power, position, and prestige do we attribute to God, our heavenly Father? What influence, wealth, and prosperity do we enjoy? What advantage is there?

There's really no comparison. God is over all. Compared with "Creator," any earthly title or position is meaningless. So don't I, as a child of my Father in heaven, enjoy great advantages? Of course! Let's list a few:

Eternal life

Who really wants this life to be all there is? And it isn't just life on earth but eternal life in heaven with God that we'll enjoy—the ultimate intimacy. Jesus told His disciples, "In My Father's house are many dwelling places … I am going away to prepare a place for you … I will come back and receive you to Myself, so that where I am you may be also" (John 14:2–3).

We'll look at heaven in more detail later, but suffice it to say for now that living eternally with God is the greatest thing that can happen.

Freedom from worry and anxiety

Anxiety is one of the great killers of our time. Worry causes and exacerbates all kinds of physical and emotional maladies, such as heart disease and depression. Contrary to the world's way, Jesus commands us not to worry (see Matthew 6:25,31,34). God supplies everything we need, so there's never a need for the Christian to worry.

Spiritual riches

Far more valuable than the world's riches, God provides true wealth. Love, joy, peace, hope, and wisdom are gifts money can never buy.

Personal power

Followers of Jesus Christ have a tremendous amount of personal power, not from our own strength but from the Holy Spirit as He lives in and through us.

There are many more advantages, but it's already clear there can be no relationship as great as being a child of God. With it, life can be full and meaningful. Without it, life falls tragically short of its true value.

The Perfect Father

Thinking back to when my children were growing up, there were times that I got it right as a father, but I have some regrets, too. I didn't always love or act the way I should have, and my children suffered for it. I realize that no earthly father will ever be perfect, and I usually tried to do my best, but I still wish I had done some things differently.

In contrast, it's comforting to know that God is always and without fail our perfect Father. He exhibits the qualities that you would expect from a perfect Father. Here are a few:

God loves.

The Bible tells us that love is God's primary attribute. In fact, God is the very source and definition of love: "Dear friends, let us love one another, because love is from God, and everyone who loves has been born of God and knows God. The one who does not love does not know God, because God is love" (1 John 4:7–8).

Since God defines love and all true love comes from God, we can examine God's love to determine how we should love.

» God's love is dependable. Isaiah witnessed to God's unshakable love for Israel: "'Though the mountains move and the hills shake, My love will not be removed from you and My covenant of peace will not be shaken,' says your compassionate Lord" (Isaiah 54:10). People are notorious for letting each other down, but God's love prohibits Him from forsaking you. David said, "But from eternity to eternity the Lord's faithful love is toward those who fear Him" (Psalm 103:17). Another Psalm says, "Give thanks to the Lord, for He is good; His faithful love endures forever" (107:1). You can always count on God's faithful love; He will never fail you.

» God's love is powerful—arguably the most powerful force in the world. Nothing can stop it, weaken it, or separate us from it. His love is powerful enough to create, sustain, redeem, and deliver us from evil. Here are three of many Bible passages that reflect the power of God's love: "Now the eye of the Lord is on those who fear Him—those who depend on His faithful love to deliver them from death and to keep them alive in famine"

(Psalm 33:18–19). "For Your faithful love is higher than the heavens; Your faithfulness reaches the clouds" (Psalm 108:4). "For I am persuaded that neither death nor life, nor angels nor rulers, nor things present, nor things to come, nor powers, nor height, nor depth, nor any other created thing will have the power to separate us from the love of God that is in Christ Jesus our Lord!" (Romans 8:38–39).

» God's love is eternal. It will never end. He will never cease to love you. You can reject God's love, but that won't stop Him from loving you. Moses told the children of Israel, "Know that Yahweh your God is God, the faithful God who keeps His gracious covenant loyalty for a thousand generations with those who love Him and keep His commands" (Deuteronomy 7:9). David sang, "Give thanks to the Lord, for He is good; His faithful love endures forever" (1 Chronicles 16:34).

So God's love makes Him the perfect Father. But some people never had a kind, loving father. Perhaps their father wasn't around much or maybe not at all. Other fathers are mean, selfish, and abusive, and their children wish their father wasn't present. If your father wasn't what he should have been, it may be difficult for you to conceive of a Father who loves perfectly. Some of us grew up never experiencing the kind of love that Paul described: "Love is patient; love is kind. Love does not envy; is not boastful; is not conceited; does not act improperly; is not selfish; is not provoked; does not keep a record of wrongs; finds no joy in unrighteousness, but rejoices in the truth; bears all things, believes all things, hopes all things, endures all things. Love never ends" (1 Corinthians 13:4–8).

God's love is all that and more, and consistently so, and it is the basis for all of His other fatherly attributes.

God is gracious, merciful, and forgiving.

Do you understand the difference between mercy and grace? Mercy is when God doesn't give us what we deserve. We deserve punishment for our sin, but when we trust in Jesus, God takes away that punishment; He exercises His mercy.

In contrast, grace happens when God does give us what we don't deserve. When He restores our relationship with Him, gives us eternal life, and helps us become more like Christ daily, He's exhibiting His grace. The connection is that both mercy and grace flow from God's wonderful love.

The Bible confirms that because of God's love, grace, and mercy, He is willing and able to forgive us when we ask. "If we confess our sins, He is faithful and righteous to forgive us our sins and to cleanse us from all unrighteousness" (1 John 1:9).

God teaches and corrects.

God is always "Teacher of the Year." He instructs us in the truth, using the Bible, prayer, music, sermons, life situations, books, examples from nature, and many other methods. If we seek Him, He is abundantly willing to teach us.

Sometimes we have to learn what is true by recognizing that what we had believed is actually false. That's God correcting us. Jesus urges us to sit in His school: "All of you, take up My yoke and learn from Me, because I am gentle and humble in heart, and you will find rest for yourselves" (Matthew 11:29).

God guides and disciplines.

God can provide daily, hourly, even minute-by-minute guidance for us in any situation. His wisdom enables us to take the right path if we depend on it. We frequently take our own selfish tack instead and experience the negative consequences, but that just confirms God was right all along. If we persist in our disobedience, God sometimes has to discipline us.

It may seem strange to include discipline in this list of attributes of a perfect father. When we hear the word "discipline," most of us usually think punishment. But the true meaning of discipline is to teach or train. Sometimes discipline is enjoyable, but it can involve pain. God disciplines us because He wants us to grow to be more like Jesus. When we go the wrong direction, He desires to steer us back on course.

There are some fathers who fail to discipline their children because they don't want them to feel bad. There are others who are too busy punishing to really discipline their children appropriately. A father who truly loves his children won't do either because he knows that love always seeks the best, and being either too lenient or too severe leads to something other than the best. God's discipline is always for our best.

God is always present and available.

God is not an absentee father. If you rarely or never saw your father, you can count on God to be different. He is always available. Psalm 145:18 confirms that "the Lord is near all who call out to Him, all who call out to Him with integrity."

It's great to realize that God is never preoccupied or annoyed. He's never too busy or too tired. In no way is God the unapproachable bully that some people imagine. Instead, He's always ready to help us when we come to Him in prayer. God welcomes, accepts, and embraces us with His undying love.

We could go on to talk about God's giving nature, patience, help in time of need, and many other attributes; the list would be long. But we'll examine some of these later, and we've seen enough for now to know that, because of His great love, God deserves to be called Father.

You: God's Child

The first recorded words of Jesus confirm that He was focused on His Father and their relationship: "'Why were you searching for Me?' He asked them. 'Didn't you know that I had to be in my Father's house?'" (Luke 2:49). Whenever the gospels record Jesus praying, He invariably addressed God as Father (see Matthew 11:25, Luke 22:42, and John 11:41 for examples). Jesus knew God first and foremost as Father.

With God as the perfect Father, who wouldn't want to be His child? Fortunately He made that possible through Jesus, of whom John says,

"He came to His own, and His own people did not receive Him. But to all who did receive Him, He gave them the right to be children of God, to those who believe in His name, who were born, not of blood, or of the will of the flesh, or of the will of man, but of God" (John 1:11–13).

Some will say that we are all God's children. In one sense that's true because He creates everything and everyone. He gives life to every person. But as we noted previously, everyone has broken his or her relationship with God by sinning (i.e., by disobeying God's laws and commands). In a way, it's like we have disowned God as our Father. Because of that choice, no one is God's child by default and certainly not through his or her own effort.

The passage above tells us that to those who believe in Jesus, God has given the right to become His children, be born into His family, and relate to Him as Father. Jesus likened this process to a new birth: "I assure you: Unless someone is born again, he cannot see the kingdom of God" (John 3:3). Paul compared it to being adopted: "All those led by God's Spirit are God's sons. For you did not receive a spirit of slavery to fall back into fear, but you received the Spirit of adoption, by whom we cry out, 'Abba, Father!' The Spirit Himself testifies together with our spirit that we are God's children" (Romans 8:14–16).

The other side of the coin is that those who do not believe in Jesus are not God's children. The cold, hard fact is that we can come to God only through Jesus. He made that abundantly clear: "Enter through the narrow gate. For the gate is wide and the road is broad that leads to destruction, and there are many who go through it. How narrow is the gate and difficult the road that leads to life, and few find it ... Not everyone who says to Me, 'Lord, Lord!' will enter the kingdom of heaven, but only the one who does the will of My Father in heaven" (Matthew 7:13–14,21).

Jesus even told the Pharisees that their father was neither Abraham nor God but Satan.

> If you were Abraham's children, you would do what
> Abraham did. But now you are trying to kill Me, a

man who has told you the truth that I heard from God. Abraham did not do this! You're doing what your father does … If God were your Father, you would love Me, because I came from God and I am here. For I didn't come on My own, but He sent Me. Why don't you understand what I say? Because you cannot listen to My word. You are of your father the Devil, and you want to carry out your father's desires. (John 8:39–44)

The inescapable conclusion is that some people become children of God and some do not. One purpose of this book is to encourage you to become God's child. If you've never experienced God's love, mercy, forgiveness, and grace, that's the most important step you can take. Everything in the Christian life is based on that relationship. (See the appendix for more information about how to do that.)

Loving God as Your Heavenly Father

When you think of God's great love and all that comes from it, it's easy to see that He truly deserves your love in return—and your love is what God desires. He wants you to be one with Him, to experience true intimacy. Since He made you for a love relationship, you are fulfilling that purpose when you love Him. It's perfectly analogous to human parents who love their child and, more than anything else, want the child's love in return.

That analogy can help us understand how choosing to love God will play out in our lives. Two primary ways that a child loves his parents are to honor and obey them. Just like a child who loves his human parents, if we love God, we will honor and obey Him.

If you love God, you will honor Him.

Beginning with the Ten Commandments, the Bible tells us to honor our parents: "Honor your father and your mother so that you may have a long life in the land that the Lord your God is giving you" (Exodus 20:12).

Honoring our parents means that we respect them, pay attention to them, defer to them, and give them credit for the things they have done for us. We honor God the same way. Of course, there is a qualitative difference in how we honor God; for example, we worship Him as Creator of the whole world. But the principle is still the same. Because we love our Father we want to give Him honor and respect. We'll take up this topic in detail in chapter 5.

If you love God, you will obey Him.

Like a child who loves his parents and wants to obey them, you will want to obey your heavenly Father. That doesn't mean you won't ever sin (what, do you think you're perfect?), but your overwhelming desire will be to please God by doing what He says.

As Jesus talked with His disciples in the upper room just before His arrest, He made a connection between love and obedience: "If you love Me, you will keep My commandments ... The one who has My commands and keeps them is the one who loves Me ... If anyone loves Me, he will keep My word ... The one who doesn't love Me will not keep My words ... As the Father has loved Me, I have also loved you. Remain in My love. If you keep My commands you will remain in My love, just as I have kept My Father's commands and remain in His love" (John 14:15,21,23–24; 15:9–10).

It should be pretty clear from those statements that loving God and obeying God are synonymous. You can't do one without the other. If you really love God, you won't mind obeying. You'll do it gladly because you know that God's laws are for your good. John reinforced this concept: "This is how we know that we love God's children when we love God and obey His commands. For this is what love for God is: to keep His commands. Now His commands are not a burden" (1 John 5:2–3).

Since God's love compels us to obey His commandments, it's important for us to study the Bible to learn them. Here are a few prime examples:

- » The Ten Commandments (Exodus 20:1–17)
- » The Greatest Commandment (Mark 12:30)
- » The Great Commission (Matthew 28:19–20)
- » Love one another (John 13:34–35)
- » Love your brother (Mark 12:31)
- » Love your enemies (Matthew 5:43–45)
- » The Golden Rule (Matthew 7:12)

God also has specific commands just for you; He has tasks for you to do in His kingdom that He doesn't assign to anyone else. We'll take a look at those commands in chapter 7.

Approach Your Father with Love

When you come to God in prayer by saying "Our Father..." you are acknowledging that God is your Father, you are His child, and you are engaging in that relationship as the basis for your prayer. You are certifying that you trust in Jesus to establish and maintain that love relationship. In addition, you are telling God that you are depending on His love, mercy, grace, guidance, discipline, etc., and that you realize He wants to talk with you as much as you want to talk with Him—maybe more. In short, you are approaching God with love in return for the love He's shown to you.

What a wonderful thing! The God who created you has an infinite love for you, and He wants you to come to Him in prayer with all the love in your heart. Because love is the most powerful force in the world and that love is the basis for our prayer, absolutely nothing can keep us from seeking God at any time, in any place or situation, for any need or desire.

It's truly unfortunate that so many people resign themselves to a life without God when He is so imminently available. Since you know the truth, don't hesitate to turn to God in prayer. Seek true intimacy with Him.

Praying to Your Perfect Father

Here are some ideas for relating to God as your heavenly Father when you pray:

» Find a time and place when you can be alone with God with no interruptions. Imagine that He is sitting right beside you, ready to engage in conversation. Begin talking as you would if you could see God sitting beside you. Try to hear what He says in response.

» The relationship that some Christians have with God is influenced by their relationship with their earthly father. Consider how God is different from your earthly father and discuss with Him how that might change your relationship for the better.

» Study God's fatherly attributes as described in the Bible and consider how each one affects your daily life. Thank God for His Fatherly acts.

» Ask God to draw you closer in a loving Father-child relationship and to help you experience true intimacy with Him.

CHAPTER SUMMARY

» There are tremendous advantages to being a child of God.

» God deserves to be called Father because He loves us supremely.

» Our heavenly Father deserves to be loved, honored, and obeyed.

» Main point: God is your ever-present, always-loving Father, so you must come to Him in prayer with love.

Pursuing Perfect* Passion

For personal or group study

1. Do you have a relationship with God? Is He truly your Father? If so, how are the advantages of that relationship (eternal life, freedom from worry, etc.) playing out in your life? If not, what's keeping you from accepting His love for you? See the appendix for a brief description of how you can become God's child.

2. Consider your earthly father. In what ways is/was he like your heavenly Father? In what ways is/was he different? How does your relationship with your earthly father help you understand and appreciate your relationship with your heavenly Father?

3. Which of God's attributes (love, grace, mercy, etc.) is most important to you at this time in your life? What's the reason behind your answer? Which of His attributes do you feel you need to understand and experience more than you are currently?

4. How fully are you experiencing God's love in your life? Do you sense His love for you on a daily basis? How intimate would you say is your relationship with your perfect Father?

5. Do you agree that God's love is the basis for His other fatherly attributes? If so, briefly describe how His love underlies each of these attributes: grace, mercy, teacher, discipline, always present. If not, what do you think is the basis for those attributes?

6. Can you remember a time when God disciplined you? What was the reason for the discipline? What were the results? Did this experience bring you closer to God or seem to separate you more?

7. Read Psalm 103 and make two lists from it: God's attributes found in this psalm and actions God performs on our behalf. Which list best matches God's relationship with you?

8. How comfortable are you with the Bible's position that not every person becomes God's child? Does that position cause you to look at other people differently? Does it cause you to have more concern for the people with whom you come in contact?

9. Does your love for God match your obedience to His commands? Could someone tell how much you love God by observing your actions? If not, what can you do to make them more congruent?

3

GOD: YOUR EXALTED KING

Our Father in heaven.
—Matthew 6:9

Now that we know God is our perfect Father, we also want to examine the "in heaven" part of our prayer salutation. These words distinguish our heavenly Father from our earthly father, but there must be more to it than that. Other than the obvious—God is in heaven—what does Jesus mean by this phrase, and how does it impact our prayer?

What and where is heaven anyway? We hear about streets of gold. We see cartoons depicting angels who pass the time by sitting on clouds playing harps, occasionally peering down and marveling at our folly. We're told that St. Peter stands at the pearly gates, solemnly checking his book to see whether the anxious soul cowering before him will be allowed into heaven or unceremoniously shuttled off to hell. Are those accurate images?

We hear of people who have died, gone to heaven, and come back minutes later by some medical miracle to tell us what they experienced.

Can we depend on those descriptions? Can we really know anything about heaven before making the trip ourselves?

Heaven: God's Perfect Residence

Heaven is outside our realm of physical existence (the universe), so the only things we can know about heaven are what God tells us. Fortunately, God has revealed a few things about heaven in the Bible.

Heaven is where God lives.

God made heaven for Himself and for those that He chooses to be there with Him. "The Lord looks down from heaven; He observes everyone. He gazes on all the inhabitants of the earth from His dwelling place" (Psalm 33:13–14). "But Stephen, filled by the Holy Spirit, gazed into heaven. He saw God's glory, with Jesus standing at the right hand of God" (Acts 7:55).

This is the main point we should understand about heaven. Once we realize that it is God's dwelling, everything else about heaven is a logical conclusion. First, it isn't a physical place but a spiritual one, since "God is spirit" (John 4:24). It must be a place of utmost beauty since God Himself is there. Heaven has to be perfect, since a perfect God would not live in a place that is anything less. There's never a bad day in heaven, and none of the things that cause pain and problems in this world. As John described, "He will wipe away every tear from their eyes. Death will exist no longer; grief, crying, and pain will exist no longer, because the previous things have passed away" (Revelation 21:4).

Heaven is eternal.

That is, heaven is not temporal; it is not bound by time. Since our lives are dominated and directed by the passing of time, that's hard for us to conceive, and that's one reason heaven is such a mystery.

Heaven has none of the transitory qualities that mark our world. There's no rust, rot, or corrosion. There is a permanence about heaven that we can never experience in our physical world.

Heaven is the final destination for God's children.

We can be certain that we will continue to enjoy our relationship with God after life on earth is over, and we will experience it in His direct presence in heaven: "For the Lord Himself will descend from heaven with a shout, with the archangel's voice, and with the trumpet of God, and the dead in Christ will rise first. Then we who are still alive will be caught up together with them in the clouds to meet the Lord in the air; and so we will always be with the Lord" (1 Thessalonians 4:16–17).

In fact, Christians are already citizens of heaven while living on earth. Paul wrote, "Our citizenship is in heaven" (Philippians 3:20). That's a pivotal point in our understanding of our role as God's children. Since we are citizens of a place where we don't live, that makes us ambassadors to the place where we do live. God doesn't just take us to heaven the moment we believe, as appealing as that would be, because we are to bear witness about what He has done for us so that others can understand and believe: "Therefore, we are ambassadors for Christ; certain that God is appealing through us, we plead on Christ's behalf, 'Be reconciled to God'" (2 Corinthians 5:20).

So even though we haven't been there and it's outside our realm of existence, we know a little about heaven. But as interesting as heaven may be, we're really seeking to better understand the one who lives there. After all, we address our prayer to God, not to an impersonal heaven. The description "in heaven" helps us understand more about our Father.

The main point is that when we pray to our Father in heaven, we must realize that we are addressing the one true God, the creator, sustainer, and ruler of the universe. There is no higher authority—He is it. There is no other figure lurking in the shadows, pulling the strings. God is the king, and there is no other. And He happens to live in heaven.

What a King!

God exhibits qualities in keeping with His position as king. We've seen that He is infinite, perfect, and holy. That also makes Him completely unique. As He tells us in the Bible, "The Lord is One" (Deuteronomy 6:4). We have only one Father in heaven, and no one else is quite like Him.

In addition, God has other kingly attributes.

God is righteous and just.

This means He is morally upright and blameless. His decisions and commands are good. There is no mixture of corruption in God's nature: "The ordinances of the Lord are reliable and altogether righteous" (Psalm 19:9). "The Lord is righteous in all His ways and gracious in all His acts" (Psalm 145:17).

Because God is righteous, He is impartial, fair, and honest. We will never experience with God the type of injustice and inequity that far too often taints the decisions of our earthly rulers and judges. He doesn't take bribes, and He never acts selfishly. All of God's judgments are appropriate and consistent with His nature. Though He is merciful and forgiving and graciously gives us eternal life that we don't deserve, He is nonetheless perfectly just and will not let unforgiven sin go unpunished.

> Let the evil of the wicked come to an end, but establish the righteous. The One who examines the thoughts and emotions is a righteous God. My shield is with God, who saves the upright in heart. God is a righteous judge, and a God who executes justice every day. (Psalm 7:9–11)

God is wise.

A related quality is God's wisdom. Just like any good king, God makes wise choices. Unlike all others, every choice God makes is wise. Since God created all that exists, He understands every detail about every situation. Like everything else about God, His wisdom is infinite: "Oh, the depth of the riches both of the wisdom and the knowledge of God! How unsearchable His judgments and untraceable His ways!" (Romans 11:33).

The Bible says that Solomon had more wisdom than anyone else alive because it was a gift from God. Only an infinitely wise God could enable a man to have that level of wisdom "God gave Solomon wisdom, very great insight, and understanding as vast as the sand on the seashore. Solomon's wisdom was greater than the wisdom of all the people of the East, greater than all the wisdom of Egypt. He was wiser than anyone" (1 Kings 4:29–31).

God is sovereign.

God created all that exists, so He is sovereign over it all. That is, He has authority and power over everything that exists. Nothing is outside His jurisdiction. He is the one king whose kingdom is unlimited, so He is sovereign over all human leaders. "Everyone must submit to the governing authorities, for there is no authority except from God, and those that exist are instituted by God" (Romans 13:1).

This doesn't mean God controls everything that happens. For example, He allows you to choose your own course of action and experience the consequences of your decisions. He allows you to exercise your free will. But He can at any time and any place that He wishes take any action that He desires. And no one can prevent God from doing whatever He pleases. He is perfectly sovereign.

Exalt the King!

Because He is king, lord, and ruler, we must approach God with complete reverence in prayer. He deserves our respect, esteem, and awe. One aspect of this reverence is that most of us should spend less time talking to God in prayer and more time listening. What God has to say is undoubtedly more significant than what we can tell Him. One reason that the Model Prayer is so short may be that it gives us more time to hear God's reply. Solomon said it this way: "Do not be hasty to speak, and do not be impulsive to make a speech before God. God is in heaven and you are on earth, so let your words be few" (Ecclesiastes 5:2).

So humility is the order of the day. We are told to "approach the throne of grace with boldness" (Hebrews 4:16), but there's a difference between bold and brash. Let's remember that God "gives grace to the humble" (Proverbs 3:34). Therefore, approach God with reverence.

The Mystery of Prayer

Our Father in heaven—what powerful words! They tell me that God, the infinite creator and ruler of the entire universe, is also my loving Father. The One who is so far beyond our earthly existence actually desires an intimate relationship with me. The sheer magnitude of the contrast is mind-boggling—God is both king in heaven and my Father with me. Isaiah explained it to the Israelites this way: "For the High and Exalted One who lives forever, whose name is Holy says this: 'I live in a high and holy place, and with the oppressed and lowly of spirit, to revive the spirit of the lowly and revive the heart of the oppressed'" (Isaiah 57:15).

Can we ever truly understand the mystery of prayer? How can we, as limited human beings on earth, call on the exalted ruler of all? What could be the reason that God wants to communicate with us? In answer to these questions, there are three important conclusions that we can state at this point in our study:

» God loves you with a dependable, powerful, eternal love, so He wants to relate to you in love and communicate with you in prayer.

» Because He loves you, and in response to your faith in Jesus, God has made you to be perfect*, so you can boldly approach God's perfect heavenly throne with complete confidence that He will accept you as His child.

» God is both the transcendent creator-king and the ever-present Father; you must come to Him in prayer with reverence and love.

Child of the King, Come!

Coming to God in prayer is like stepping into His heavenly throne room with all the hosts of heaven in attendance. Just imagine! It's not some dark, foreboding castle with strange and scary creatures lurking in the shadows. God is the source of the light, and that light is shining on the heavenly host of angelic beings who are standing to serve and bowing in worship. God sees you as you enter and immediately beckons you to come to Him. He calls out, "Child of the king, come!" After all, He's your Father. You aren't just anybody—you're God's child! You can run to Him, crawl up into His lap, and talk with Him about whatever you need. Of course, you should want even more to listen as He reveals the wonderful things He has to tell you. With a Father like that, who can resist such an invitation? Come!

Praying to the Exalted King

God is your Father in heaven. He wants you to come in prayer as His child. The key is to learn to balance an intimate relationship with your loving Father with a reverential respect for your awesome king. Try these ideas to help strike that balance:

» As you pray, try to imagine God on his heavenly throne. Seek to reflect an attitude of reverence as you pray to the exalted king.

» Embark on a Bible study of God's kingly attributes. A good place to start is in Psalms. Note each characteristic you encounter and ask God to help you understand how it relates to your prayers.

» Practice silent worship in God's presence. Try kneeling or bowing as you listen to what He has to say. Imagine yourself kneeling before God on His throne and waiting on Him in reverent silence.

» On a regular basis, practice prayers in which you simply praise and worship God for who He is without making any requests. Note how much joy arises simply from praising God.

» Ask God to show you how to maintain respect for His holy presence while still drawing close to Him in love.

Chapter Summary

» Heaven is God's perfect, eternal dwelling place.

» As the infinite, perfect, holy creator, God is enthroned as the king of the universe.

» God deserves to be revered as the exalted king.

» "Our Father in heaven" is a powerful phrase that set the entire tone for the Model Prayer.

» Main point: God is the infinite and holy king, so you must come to Him in prayer with reverence.

Pursuing Perfect* Passion

For personal or group study

1. What is your concept of heaven? What do you expect it to be like? What do you not know about heaven that you wish you knew?

2. Study these Bible passages: 1 Kings 22:19–22; Nehemiah 9:5–8; Psalm 89:5–11; Isaiah 66:1–2; John 14:1–6; and Revelation 4:1–11. What do they tell you about heaven? What do they tell you about God?

3. What does it mean to you that God is perfectly righteous and just? How does His perfect justice affect your relationship with Him?

4. What is wisdom? How does your current level of wisdom compare with Solomon's? With God's? Do you think God would give you more wisdom if you asked? In your opinion, is that a valid prayer request?

5. What is your perception of God's sovereignty and how He uses it? Do you think God ever overrides your free will? Why or why not?

6. In addition to those listed in the chapter, what other kingly attributes of God can you add to the list? Of all these, which seems most applicable to your understanding of God? What's the reason for your choice?

7. Write a paragraph describing your idea of God as king of the universe. Compare and contrast your concept with the Bible's description of God. Compare and contrast God as king with earthly rulers.

8. How much of your prayer time is devoted to listening to God? If you need to increase that percentage, what practical steps can you take?

9. What do you think is God's motivation for allowing mere mortals to come to Him in prayer? What value could there be for an infinite, perfect king to allow sinful humans like us to approach His throne in prayer?

10. How well do you comprehend the combination of God as intimate, loving Father and as majestic, heavenly king? Does that association seem like a wonderful mystery or is it more mundane to you? Why?

11. Is it more important for you, at this time in your life, to relate to God as loving Father or as exalted King? What is your reason?

4

PASSION: THE HEART OF THE MATTER

Love the Lord your God with all your heart, with all your
soul, with all your mind, and with all your strength.
—Mark 12:30

ROMEO AND JULIET LOVED PASSIONATELY enough to die for one another. Martin Luther King, Jr. was passionate about justice and civil rights. Perhaps the greatest physicist of all time, Albert Einstein famously said, "I have no special talents. I am only passionately curious." Charles Wesley was so passionate about Christ that he wrote more than eight thousand hymns.

Are you passionate? Do you abound with vitality and excitement? Are you constantly on the go? Even if you aren't, you probably know some people like that. They commonly take on roles like actor, salesman, or cheerleader. These are the people who are always enthusiastic, always excited, always "up"—the "rah-rah" people who get folks fired up about whatever there is to be fired up about. The more energy they burn, the more they have; it seems they never run out.

But is that what we really mean when we use the word "passion"? Enthusiasm and excitement? Fireworks and flash?

True passion is less about excitement than energy. The heart of passion is a burning desire to achieve a goal, accomplish an end, or realize a result. It doesn't always have to be an adrenaline rush of activity. Passion is the strong, enduring push that drives one to the finish. Thomas Edison exhibited this kind of passion when he tried countless materials while developing a useful light bulb. Passion drove Christopher Columbus to discover and explore the new world. William Wilberforce passionately worked his entire adult life to end slavery in the British Empire. These men weren't looking for an exhilarating experience; they were pursuing a purpose.

Passion isn't so much fire as it is desire. Passion is the inner drive needed to propel your life to where it needs to go. Let's face it—nothing important happens in this world without passion. It is the source of every beautiful song, work of art, successful business, and relationship that produces a family. Every meaningful activity and accomplishment begins with some kind of passion, desire, or drive to make something happen, create something lasting, or defend a cause. We need passion to live life to its fullest.

Then what is our source of passion? Our lives must be driven by something. Is it obedience to God's commands? As important as it is, obedience is a result, not a cause. Does our passion come from a sense of purpose? Sure, purpose gives us direction, but many great purposes go unrealized. How about a sacrificial giving of one's self? Sacrifice can be heroic, but it won't provide the daily drive we need to live our lives.

There's nothing wrong with any of these; in fact, Jesus exhibited all of them to the utmost. Obedience, purpose, and sacrifice are true marks of the Christian life. By themselves, however, none of these will provide the burning desire that a follower of Christ needs to live a full, abundant life. Our source of passion must be the most fundamental aspect of our relationship with God. Thus, the heart of the matter is love—God's love for you and your love in response.

God Loves You Passionately

We've already seen that love is God's primary attribute. God loves everyone, including you. One classic example of God's love is the parable of the prodigal son. Jesus told of a younger brother who demanded what he had coming to him: "A man had two sons. The younger of them said to his father, 'Father, give me the share of the estate I have coming to me.' So he distributed the assets to them. Not many days later, the younger son gathered together all he had and traveled to a distant country, where he squandered his estate in foolish living. After he had spent everything, a severe famine struck that country, and he had nothing" (Luke 15:11–14).

Here we see a foolish young man apparently determined to destroy all of his family relationships in one fell swoop. Obviously intending to leave home for a life of revelry, he demands his share of his father's estate. Normally, a child doesn't receive a share of the estate until his father dies. So in a sense this man was telling his father, "I no longer want to live here with you. I'm out of here. I'm going to live my own life, so give me my share now. As far as I'm concerned, you're dead." What a cruel and cutting message, and how hurt his father must have been.

Unfortunately, we're just like that younger son. Our human nature wants to live life on our terms, not in obedience to God or anyone else. We are by nature rebellious and self-sufficient. It may not always be so overt, but we are self-serving enough to want what we think is ours so we can spend it on our own desires. This approach to life is self-defeating, of course, and if we are wise we mature beyond it.

But the one we really hurt is God. As we thumb our noses at Him in our rearview mirror, we don't realize that what we see is a Father who, while cut to the heart, still loves us with an infinite passion.

In the story, as the prodigal son wastes his possessions and ends up practically a slave, the father continues to wait, searching the horizon day after day for any sign of his son returning. While he still has his older son (the self-righteous one) with him, his heart goes out to his lost younger son. Eventually, he sees him.

> So he got up and went to his father. But while the son was still a long way off, his father saw him and was filled with compassion. He ran, threw his arms around his neck, and kissed him. The son said to him, "Father, I have sinned against heaven and in your sight. I'm no longer worthy to be called your son."
>
> But the father told his slaves, "Quick! Bring out the best robe and put it on him; put a ring on his finger and sandals on his feet. Then bring the fattened calf and slaughter it, and let's celebrate with a feast, because this son of mine was dead and is alive again; he was lost and is found!" (Luke 15:20–24)

What love! What passion! What a burning desire that father had! This story could be called, as someone has said, the parable of the loving father.

The point of the story is that no matter what you have done, where you have been, or what you have experienced, God still loves you passionately, and His greatest desire is an intimate love relationship with you. Each of us is the prodigal son, and God is the loving, forgiving father. His heart goes out to you as He's constantly searching the horizon, waiting for you to come home to Him.

Jesus committed the ultimate act of love when He willingly endured death on the cross to pay for our sins. By doing so, He made it possible for us to experience the intimate relationship with God that He wants and that we need. Of course, His heavenly Father allowed Him to die on the cross, even though God loved His Son, because He loves us too. Here's a sampling what the Bible says about God's love and Jesus' sacrifice:

» "God's love was revealed among us in this way: God sent His One and Only Son into the world so that we might live through

Him. Love consists in this: not that we loved God, but that He loved us and sent His Son to be the propitiation for our sins" (1 John 4:9–10).

» "No one has greater love than this, that someone would lay down his life for his friends" (John 15:13).

» "For rarely will someone die for a just person—though for a good person perhaps someone might even dare to die. But God proves His own love for us in that while we were still sinners Christ died for us!" (Romans 5:7–8).

» "And walk in love, as the Messiah also loved us and gave Himself for us, a sacrificial and fragrant offering to God" (Ephesians 5:2).

» "This is how we have come to know love: He laid down His life for us. We should also lay down our lives for our brothers" (1 John 3:16).

God isn't just willing to have an intimate, loving relationship with you—He *desires* it. He created you for that reason. He will stop at nothing to woo you into that relationship. The king of the universe loves you and wants your love in return. It doesn't matter who you are, where you are, what you've done, or where you're headed. God loves you passionately!

Who Do You Love?

It's not just a classic song by Bo Diddley. It's a crucial question. As human beings we love many different people and things. We love our family members, friends, and maybe some others—usually the people who are most important to us. There are extreme examples, such as Mother Teresa, who love everyone they encounter and give themselves for them.

We also love certain things and activities: possessions, wealth, power, merrymaking, leisure, sports, fame, and socializing, just to name a few. It's human nature to love the people, things, and activities that are important to us.

Jesus made it very clear, however, that our greatest passion—our greatest love—must be for God. While in Jerusalem for Passover, He was asked about God's foremost commandment:

> One of the scribes approached. When he heard them debating and saw that Jesus answered them well, he asked Him, "Which commandment is the most important of all?"
>
> "This is the most important," Jesus answered: "Listen, Israel! The Lord our God, the Lord is One. Love the Lord your God with all your heart, with all your soul, with all your mind, and with all your strength.
>
> "The second is: Love your neighbor as yourself. There is no other commandment greater than these."
>
> Then the scribe said to Him, "You are right, Teacher! You have correctly said that He is One, and there is no one else except Him. And to love Him with all your heart, with all your understanding, and with all your strength, and to love your neighbor as yourself, is far more important than all the burnt offerings and sacrifices."
>
> When Jesus saw that he answered intelligently, He said to him, "You are not far from the kingdom of God." (Mark 12:28–34)

The chief priests, scribes, elders, Pharisees, Herodians, and Sadducees had already tested Jesus with questions designed to trick Him, but they had all failed (see Mark 11:27–12:27). What an astounding group of people! In today's world, that would be like the president, the Supreme

Court, the Republicans, the Democrats, the Green Party, the Tea Party, the imperialists, the isolationists, the Rotary Club, and a few Rastafarians. Throw in Boss Hogg and Sheriff Rosco P. Coltrane to boot.

These people had many disagreements, but they had one thing in common: they all had a bone to pick with Jesus. They wanted to ridicule, silence, arrest, or kill Him—whatever it took to get Him out of their hair.

Why all this animosity? Why were they so concerned about one itinerant preacher who by all reports seemed to be helping a whole lot of people? It was because Jesus threatened their way of life. When Jesus spoke, "All the people were captivated by what they heard" (Luke 19:48). He was drawing all the attention away from these leaders. He had criticized them throughout His ministry because they refused to lead with love and compassion. Then Jesus had the gall to come and cleanse the temple of all the moneychangers and vendors! He was shaking the very foundation of their position in Israel, and they aimed to put a stop to it, no matter what!

Then along came a scribe who, in contrast to all the others, seemed to actually seek an answer from Jesus. He wanted to know what Jesus considered to be the most important commandment of all from God. No doubt that was a frequent topic of debate among the scribes. Their job was to interpret the Jewish law, both in the courts and everyday situations, so knowing the most important point of law would be vital. What's amazing is that, in this toxic environment in which almost every other leader wanted Jesus' head, one single scribe had an honest question.

Jesus responded by quoting Deuteronomy 6:4–5 and Leviticus 19:18. He said that love is the most important commandment. First, love God. Second, love others. He wasn't giving some brand-new command. These were God's most important laws all along. Over hundreds of years the Jews had replaced God's priorities with their own legalistic rituals. Jesus pointed out that they needed to get back to what God cares about most: love.

What does it really mean to love God "with all your heart"? Jesus didn't mean the fist-sized muscle in your chest, but like the physical heart that pumps life-sustaining blood through the body, your heart is what drives and sustains your life. It's the seat of your emotions, inner drive and desire, the foundation of who and what you are as an individual. Like the boiler of a steamship or the reactor of a nuclear submarine, it's what makes everything happen—the inner core of your being.

The heart was described this way frequently in the Old Testament. Moses repeatedly encouraged the children of Israel to "love the Lord your God and worship Him with all your heart and all your soul" (Deuteronomy 11:13). When God guided Samuel to select David as Israel's king, He said that "man sees what is visible, but the Lord sees the heart" (1 Samuel 16:7). When King David later repented of his sin, he asked God to "create a clean heart for me" (Psalm 51:10). So when Moses told the Israelites to "love the Lord your God with all your heart," he meant to love God with all you are and all you have and all you hope to be—with your past, present, and future. Leaving room for absolutely no exceptions, love God in any and all situations, on each and every day of your life, with one hundred percent of your capacity to love. By loving God in this way, you make God your true passion in life.

The Heart is First

Jesus didn't say to love God with just your heart, but he did list it first. One might think that the soul or spirit should come before the heart. After all, we're spiritual beings whose spirits within us can communicate directly with God's spirit. But it is your heart that directs and drives everything you do, including what your spirit does. So the heart comes first. God wants you to have a heart like His and love Him with all your heart.

It's just like a man who loves his wife with all his heart. He won't be unfaithful by involving himself physically or emotionally with another woman; he'd much rather devote himself to his wife because she is his heart's first love. That's why it's a matter of the heart. All these other things are important, but the heart comes first. If you truly love God with all your heart, then your soul, mind, and strength will follow.

Jesus honored the scribe's integrity by quoting the foremost commandment (love God) and then added the second one (love others) as a bonus. And the scribe was in complete agreement. His last comment was most unusual. To say that loving God is more important than the established Jewish rituals could have been labeled blasphemy by the other leaders. One can well imagine that the next morning's scribal council was in a frenzy about this rogue's sympathizing ways.

Jesus also noted that this particular scribe wasn't far from being in God's true kingdom. That is, he had the right attitude, mindset, and belief to understand that God's kingdom was all about a loving relationship with his heavenly Father, and that is much more important than fulfilling all of the legal requirements that the earthly leaders had heaped up.

God Loves First

It's important to note that God loves us first. Think about it: God created you, sustains your life, and redeems you through Christ's sacrifice. He also gives purpose to your life, priority to your work, protection from harm, and many other things. He took the initiative. He made all of the first moves. It's up to you to respond in love. John said, "We love because He first loved us" (1 John 4:19).

The loving father didn't wait for his prodigal son to learn to discipline himself, make restitution for the money he'd wasted, or even finish his apology. He loved his son all along and was just waiting for him to come back home. God, with an infinite capacity to love, has loved us in so many ways. Once we begin to realize the magnitude of God's passion, we begin to desire to love God in return. God had the passion for us first, and we learn to respond with passion for God. God's love is the source of our love for Him.

A husband and wife are to love each other no matter what. They vow to have and hold, for better or worse, for richer or poorer, in sickness or health, for as long as they both live. Similarly, no matter what happens, I can believe that God loves me and thus is always acting in my best interest—whatever God leads me into or out of, whatever He gives me or withholds from me, whatever He saves me from or allows me to endure. I must never lose faith or stop loving God. I might question Him or wonder what His grand scheme entails, but I must realize that God is in charge, so I can love Him and keep going no matter what.

I love my wife, Mary, with all my heart. If I say that and then carouse with some other woman, do I really love Mary with all my heart? Of course not! If I put some other woman before her, that's infidelity. In the same way, if I allow something or someone to come between me and God, I'm being unfaithful to God and not loving Him with all my heart.

How Will You Know?

Your passion for God will have clear results. If you truly love God with all your heart, soul, mind, and strength, it will be obvious to anyone who's watching. According to Dr. Gary Chapman, God expresses His love for us in many different ways, but "we tend to express our love [for God] in our primary love language."[2] Dr. Chapman says we always express love in one of five "love languages": words of affirmation, receiving gifts, acts of service, quality time, and physical touch. If my primary love language is words of affirmation, for example, I may express love for God mainly through prayers of praise and thanksgiving. If it's acts of service, I'll seek ministry opportunities to others. Regardless of your primary love language, however, you will exhibit certain specific indicators of your love for God.

If you love God fully, you will spend time with Him.
When a boy falls head over heels in love with a girl whom he's just met, he can't get enough time with her. She's the most beautiful thing in the world. Everything she does is wonderful; nothing she does is wrong.

---

2   Gary D. Chapman, *Love Languages of God* (Chicago: Northfield, 2002), 118.

We call this state infatuation. He skips ball practice, skips school, misses meals, ignores his friends—whatever he has to do to spend time with this girl, he's going to do it. Eventually, if the relationship begins to grow into real love, he still wants to spend time with her, but it's no longer just for the physical desire to be near her. It's because he wants to share life with her. That's the beginning of mature love.

Your love relationship with God is similar. Sometimes when a person first becomes a Christian he experiences "spiritual infatuation." He is so overjoyed with the liberating feeling of being saved that he wants to do everything he can to be close to God: learn about Him by studying the Bible, take part in prayer groups, attend worship services and Christian music concerts, and talk about God incessantly. Sometimes, especially to his unsaved friends, it may seem like he is going overboard.

As the Christian's relationship with God begins to deepen into real love, he still wants to spend time with God, but it's not just because of the excitement. It becomes a desire to know God better, understand Him, serve Him, and obey Him. He still wants to spend time with God, but it's a deep desire that is spawned from the love he has for God.

We need to realize that, more than doing things for God, He wants us to spend time being with Him. That's part of what intimacy and oneness mean—being together. Jesus named twelve men as apostles "to be with Him" (Mark 3:14). God repeatedly summoned Moses to Mount Sinai to be with Him. Throughout the wilderness journey He met with Moses at the tent of meeting outside the Israelite camp. Joshua, Moses' assistant, didn't want to even leave the tent (see Exodus 33:11). Samuel, David, and many others spent a lot of time just being in the presence of God.

Since spending time with God is so important, how does one do that? Here's a partial list:

- » Personal prayer and meditation
- » Personal Bible study
- » Family worship time

- » Corporate worship services
- » Reading Christian books
- » Listening to Christian music
- » Memorizing Bible verses

If your primary love language is quality time, you may find it easy to devote time to God. For the rest of us, it may be more difficult to do things like get up early in the morning to have a quiet time. Does such a person not love God with all their heart? No, it just means that that person's preference is to express love for God in other ways.

If that's you, consider the value of starting out the day by spending just a few minutes with God. Invariably I've found that when I don't get up early and listen to His voice, it's a lot more difficult to understand what God is saying to me throughout the rest of the day. The majority of what I hear from God is what He tells me early in the morning. I believe that real love for God will result in a desire to meet Him first thing every day. Jesus is our best example: "Very early in the morning, while it was still dark, He got up, went out, and made His way to a deserted place. And He was praying there" (Mark 1:35).

Regardless of the time of day, just like a human love relationship, our love for God will be marked by spending as much time together as possible. We will do all we can to seek Him in prayer, listen to Him, and understand Him. We will tell God that we love Him and prove it by spending time with Him. We will become more intimate with Him by drawing close to Him on a very regular basis. As James said, "Draw near to God, and He will draw near to you" (James 4:8).

If you love God fully, you will become like Jesus.

You may have a WWJD bracelet. They became popular among Christian youth in the 1990s, WWJD being an acronym for "What Would Jesus Do?" The point was that Jesus always treated people with love and compassion, so we should want to do the same by following His example.

After washing His disciples' feet, Jesus told them, "I have given you an example that you also should do just as I have done for you" (John 13:15). John points out that "the one who says he remains in Him should walk just as He walked" (1 John 2:6). That means that we should show love, kindness, mercy, and forgiveness to others. Jesus "went about doing good" (Acts 10:38), and we should do the same.

But it goes beyond that. We are to be like Jesus not only by our loving actions but also by enduring persecution. Jesus said, "If anyone wants to come with Me, he must deny himself, take up his cross daily, and follow Me" (Luke 9:23). Peter pointed out that believers are "called to this, because Christ also suffered for you, leaving you an example, so that you should follow in His steps" (1 Peter 2:21). Paul told Timothy that "all those who want to live a godly life in Christ Jesus will be persecuted" (2 Timothy 3:12).

The reality is that the world is not kind toward Christians, and those in some countries have painful first-hand awareness of that fact. Christians in the United States have little experience with real suffering for Christ, but when it comes we should embrace it. Paul said it this way:

> But everything that was a gain to me, I have considered to be a loss because of Christ. More than that, I also consider everything to be a loss in view of the surpassing value of knowing Christ Jesus my Lord. Because of Him I have suffered the loss of all things and consider them filth, so that I may gain Christ and be found in Him, not having a righteousness of my own from the law, but one that is through faith in Christ—the righteousness from God based on faith. My goal is to know Him and the power of His resurrection and the fellowship of His sufferings, being conformed to His death, assuming that I will somehow reach the resurrection from among the dead. (Philippians 3:7–11)

It's a common perception that married couples, over time, begin to look more and more alike. Similarly, as you grow more intimate with

God, you will become more like Jesus, through both good times and bad, in triumphs and trials, enjoying the rewards and enduring the hardships. Through it all, God will transform you into the likeness of Christ. "For those He foreknew He also predestined to be conformed to the image of His Son, so that He would be the firstborn among many brothers" (Romans 8:29).

If you love God fully, you will adopt His perspective.

Since God is perfect, He sees everything with the proper perspective. He observes people, events, and actions and judges them appropriately. As we love God and as He transforms us into the likeness of Jesus, we will learn to see the world just like He does.

God loves people. He loves you and your neighbor. God sees each person as worthy of His infinite love. That's why the second greatest commandment, according to Jesus, is to love your neighbor. John stated it clearly: "If anyone says, 'I love God,' yet hates his brother, he is a liar. For the person who does not love his brother whom he has seen cannot love God whom he has not seen. And we have this command from Him: the one who loves God must also love his brother" (1 John 4:20–21).

God loves people, but He isn't always so pleased with what people do. As we've already seen, when we disobey God we are sinning, and God abhors sin. Hence the old saying, "God hates the sin but loves the sinner." When we have God's perspective, we'll hate sin too, whether it's our own sin or someone else's. Hating sin but loving the person who commits that sin isn't normal by the world's standards. That's why we need God's perspective.

Finally, loving God means not loving the world and by that we mean the material things and pleasures that the world offers. Things by themselves are not inherently evil. After all, God knows that we need some things to live and willingly provides them for us. But when we put desire for things and activities above our desire for God, we have the wrong perspective. "Do not love the world or the things that belong to the world. If anyone loves the world, love for the Father is not in him.

Because everything that belongs to the world—the lust of the flesh, the lust of the eyes, and the pride in one's lifestyle—is not from the Father, but is from the world" (1 John 2:15–16).

If you fully love God, you will desire to spend time with Him, grow to be like Jesus, and see people and things as God sees them. As we continue, we will see that in addition to these three, there are many other ways in which our love for God expresses itself.

It's Your Move

One can just imagine Jesus holding up His thumb and forefinger and saying to the scribe, "You are this close to the kingdom!" True, the scribe was standing right next to Him, but that wasn't what Jesus meant. He was saying that the scribe was close in heart to God and thus was close to believing in Jesus. He understood that love is the key to having a true relationship with God the Father.

God desired intimacy with the scribe based on His love for him. Similarly, God is calling you into a deep and intimate relationship, and that intimacy with Him is what you should be seeking above all else.

Where are you? Are you this close to the kingdom? Don't go into eternity this close to believing in Jesus. By putting your faith in Him, you can establish a love relationship with God that will last forever. Go all the way into the kingdom. God's love is infinite, persistent, and compelling. Don't wait any longer. Respond to His love with all your heart. Realize that loving God is all that matters. Once you do that, everything else—literally everything else—will fall into place properly. God's passionate love for you, and your passion for God in return, form the strongest foundation for your prayers.

Praying with Passion

Here are some ways to build intimacy with God by learning to pray with passion:

» Thank God for His supreme love for you, and ask Him to help you love Him supremely.

» Express daily appreciation to Jesus for His willing sacrifice on the cross on your behalf.

» Meditate on the things about which you are passionate. Ask God to make Him your greatest passion in life.

» Ask God what it means to be intimate with Him and listen carefully for His answer. Seek to build that intimacy daily.

» Determine how much of your time in a typical day is spent with God. Ask God to help you evaluate whether that is sufficient.

» Develop the habit of praying daily during the time of day at which you function best.

» Ask God to transform your heart and mind to become like Jesus.

» Compare your perspective on people and things with God's view. Ask for help to change your perspective to be more like His.

Chapter Summary

» Passion supplies the energy you need to live life to the fullest.

» God loves you passionately and desires a passionate love relationship with you.

» You are to love God passionately above all else, including yourself, others, and the world.

» Your passion for God will result in a desire to spend time with Him, continual growth to be like Jesus, and a perspective just like God's.

» Main point: Your love for God is to be the passion that drives all parts of your life, including your prayers.

Pursuing Perfect* Passion

For personal or group study

1. What does passion mean to you? About whom or what are you passionate?

2. In what ways does your heart influence the actions of your soul, mind, and strength? Is your heart really the epicenter of your passion?

3. What evidence from your life's history indicates that God has passionately loved you? How does God's passionate love for you show up in your current circumstances?

4. How passionate are you for God? Do you have an intimate, passionate love relationship?

5. It is said that in a good marriage the partners say "I love you" at least once daily. When is the last time that you told God that you love Him? How sincere are you when you say it?

6. The chapter outlined three results of a passion for God:

   » A desire to spend time with Him

   » A desire to be like Jesus

   » A perspective that is like God's perspective

   » Evaluate your own love for God using these three criteria.

7. According to 1 John 4:18, "Perfect love drives out fear." Is having no fear a reliable indication that you love God with all your heart? In what ways has God's perfect love driven fear from your life?

8. Jesus said to "love your enemies and pray for those who persecute you." Read Matthew 5:43–48. Do you love your enemies? Have

you ever prayed for one of them? If so, how did you feel about it and what happened? Is verse 44 directly related to verse 48? That is, do we have to love and pray for our enemies to be perfect in God's eyes?

9. What is your primary love language? Consult Dr. Gary Chapman's "love language" books to discover your primary love language, and then determine how you can show love for God through that language.

10. Jesus told the scribe that he wasn't far from the kingdom of God. How far are you from His kingdom? Are you outside, very close, just barely in, or all the way in? What actions do you believe you should you take based on your answer?

Part Two

Concentrating on God in Prayer

Prayer is a conversation with God. Now that we're clear about the person with whom we are conversing, it's time to examine the topics of conversation.

When a child learns to pray, it's not unusual for his prayers to focus on multiple requests for God to give something to him, do something for him, or satisfy some other personal desire. That's normal, we think, since a child isn't expected to be mature. As we mature in our relationship with God, however, we realize that these kinds of requests can be somewhat selfish. If they continue to dominate our prayers, that can be an indication of stunted growth in the Christian life.

In contrast, God's approach is for us to begin by focusing on Him rather than on ourselves. He knows that you need to look outside yourself to become like Him, and there's no better place to look than to God Himself. Jesus certainly endorsed this way of praying, and the Model Prayer is the prime example.

The chapters in this section delve into the first three phrases, each of which begins with the word *Your*. Not *our* and not *my*. Our loving Father wants us to begin with what's most important. Since our relationship with God is founded on His love, we must begin to pray by reflecting on Him first.

5

God's Glory: Your Purpose

Your name be honored as holy.
—Matthew 6:9

A T ONE TIME MY JOB was designing and building software. It didn't take long to realize that understanding the purpose of the software was paramount when engaging in design. That frequently meant working with other people, especially the ones who were going to use the system, to find out what they needed and desired from it. This part of software design is known as "documenting the requirements," and it can be fraught with error if the designers and the users don't communicate well.

I remember one project in which I was told that the users were too busy to talk with me, so I essentially had to guess what they wanted, and—surprise, surprise—we weren't on the same mental wavelength. Needless to say, the results were far from spectacular.

Regardless of the situation, there had to be an overall purpose for the software or else it was a waste of time to build it. That's true for anything that's designed, whether it's a table, recipe, picture frame, house, golf club, bridge, shirt, or computer program. You create something for a particular purpose, and you're going to use it to achieve an end. Although something may be used for a different purpose than designed (using a wrench to drive a nail, for example) the designed object realizes its true value only by fulfilling its original purpose.

The same is true with everything that God designed, including you. When God created you, He designed you for a purpose. Yes, whether or not you realize it, God has a specific purpose for your life, and you will find the most happiness and fulfillment if you seek to achieve His purpose for you. By doing that, and not just seeking to satisfy your own desires in life, you participate in His creative act.

In this chapter we will find that God's overall purpose is the same for everyone, and that is to bring honor and glory to Him.

First Things First

The first phrase in the Model Prayer is the weightiest. God doesn't beat around the burning bush. He says up front what's most important. In the Ten Commandments, the ones about our relationship to God come first because they're the most important. When Jesus preached the Sermon on the Mount, He began by describing the distinctive qualities of believers because that was His most important topic for the day. And it's most important that we first pray that God's name be honored as holy.

Why honor God's name? Why not just say "honor God"? What's so important about His name? More so in Bible times than now, a person's name reflected the essence of his character. Children were named carefully because the meaning of their name had a big impact on their life. Here are two examples:

> » "Your name will no longer be Abram ('The Father Is Exalted'), but your name will be Abraham ('Father of a Multitude'), for I will make you the father of many nations" (Genesis 17:5).

> » "My lord should pay no attention to this worthless man Nabal,

for he lives up to his name: His name is Nabal ('Fool'), and stupidity is all he knows" (1 Samuel 25:25).

Therefore, when we honor God's name, we are honoring God, His character, His essence. Honoring God's name as holy means that we hold God's name, and therefore God, in highest esteem as the divine cause and creator of all that exists.

God is already glorified by His entire creation. He created the universe to give Himself praise. As we noted in Chapter 1, the sheer majesty of the created order screams out that God created all of this!

"The heavens declare the glory of God, and the sky proclaims the work of His hands" (Psalm 19:1). "Hallelujah! Praise the Lord from the heavens; praise Him in the heights. Praise Him, all His angels; praise Him, all His hosts. Praise Him, sun and moon; praise Him, all you shining stars. Praise Him, highest heavens, and you waters above the heavens. Let them praise the name of the Lord, for He commanded, and they were created. He set them in position forever and ever; He gave an order that will never pass away" (Psalm 148:1–6).

God designed mankind as the crown of His creation, to be foremost among the creatures that honor His name as holy. That's why Jesus made this point first. We, among all the beings that God created, should lead the way in glorifying the Creator. (Unfortunately, humans seem to lead in dishonoring God by our attitudes and actions, but that's a separate point.) When we get to heaven, we'll join the throng in glorifying God in eternity.

Then I looked, and heard the voice of many angels around the throne, and also of the living creatures, and of the elders. Their number was countless thousands, plus thousands of thousands. They said with a loud

> voice: The Lamb who was slaughtered is worthy to
> receive power and riches and wisdom and strength and
> honor and glory and blessing! I heard every creature
> in heaven, on earth, under the earth, on the sea, and
> everything in them say: Blessing and honor and glory
> and dominion to the One seated on the throne, and to
> the Lamb, forever and ever! (Revelation 5:11–13)

If this design seems selfish or arrogant on God's part, ask yourself this: who else deserves this kind of treatment? Who else is worthy of praise from all mankind? We already know that God is the only one who is:

» omnipotent—able to create the whole universe

» omniscient—knowing and understanding all that happens

» all-loving—loving each and every person on earth

God isn't acting selfishly when He commands us to worship Him. He realizes that when we glorify Him we put ourselves in the appropriate position: worshipping the One who deserves it. Instead of revering something less (money, fame, power, position) or someone less (rock star, movie star, athlete, politician), we can revere the best. Only God is perfect in every conceivable fashion and thus worthy of all honor and praise, so we are to honor God's name as holy. That's why our overall purpose—our ultimate achievement—is to glorify God.

What Does *Glorify* Really Mean?

So what does it mean to honor God's name as holy? Let's begin by defining our terms, and then we'll see what it means in a practical sense.

First let's define two key words: honor and holy. To honor God means to acknowledge, proclaim, and exemplify God's holiness.

Acknowledge God as holy.

First, you must agree that God is holy. Those who don't believe in

God or who ignore Him aren't even getting to first base because they don't accept God and His holiness. By mentally acknowledging the fact that God exists and is the holy, perfect Creator, you begin to honor Him. "Acknowledge that the Lord is God. He made us, and we are His—His people, the sheep of His pasture" (Psalm 100:3).

Proclaim God as holy.

The second aspect to honoring God is to declare. The act of telling other people about God's holiness solidifies your belief and spreads the truth around. "I will thank the Lord with all my heart; I will declare all Your wonderful works. I will rejoice and boast about You; I will sing about Your name, Most High" (Psalm 9:1–2).

Exemplify God as holy.

Finally, if you are God's child, you are to embody God's holy attributes. Though limited in scope, you can demonstrate God's holiness by living a holy life. God isn't pleased with just lip service. He desires for your whole life to glorify Him.

That's what honor means. Now, exactly what do we acknowledge, proclaim, and exemplify? That is, what does holy mean? We began the definition in Chapter 1, and we can expand on that by noting that God's holiness involves His person, presence, and power.

God's holiness involves His person.

By God's person, we mean not only His attributes and characteristics but also His very existence. We know that He is loving, gracious, merciful, righteous, just, wise, and sovereign. And His existence is the reason that anything else exists.

To describe God as holy is to describe His station as the first and foremost person of the universe, the original being from whom everything else has proceeded.

God's holiness involves His presence.

We saw earlier that, because God is our Father, He is near to us when we call on Him. His ability to be present and active in our lives sets Him apart from everyone else. His presence is holy.

God's holiness involves His power.

Tornados, lightning, hurricanes, earthquakes, tsunamis—these are powerful natural phenomena which we have no power to combat. Consider how small these are compared to the immensity of the universe, and you begin to get an inkling of the scope of God's infinite power. He created the entire universe from scratch. He has the power to sustain our lives on earth. And He has the power to save those people who trust in Him and change their lives forever. God is holy because of His uniquely infinite power.

Thus, we say that God is holy because His person, presence, and power set Him apart from everything and everyone else.

In summary, to glorify God means to acknowledge, proclaim, and exemplify God's person, presence, and power. By doing that, we honor His name as holy.

How Do You Do That?

Okay, so much for definitions. All of that sounds well and good in theory, but what does it mean in the real world? Getting down to brass tacks, how do we glorify God in a practical sense, in our everyday lives? Here are several ways:

We glorify God when we praise Him.

The Bible is filled with psalms and prayers of praise to God. We praise God when we sing praise songs, shout praise to Him, or even praise Him silently. Praise is simply a direct declaration of God's glory. By praising God, we proclaim his person, presence, and power.

We glorify God when we pray to Him.

God commands us to pray. This whole book is a commentary on the ways that Jesus teaches us to pray. Prayer is truly an acknowledgment that God is the powerful, loving God who can act on our prayers.

We glorify God when we listen to Him.

Just like a child honors his parents when he listens to them, we honor God by paying attention to the things He tells us. It brings us great value to listen to God in prayer. Listening to God's voice acknowledges His person and presence.

We glorify God when we obey Him.

To honor God, we must choose things that please Him rather than the things that please ourselves. Again, just as a child has a good idea what pleases her parents, we know the right thing to do most of the time. Obeying is one way to exemplify God's person and power.

We glorify God when we spend time with Him.

God chose you to be His child because He wants an intimate relationship with you. Spending time together is vital to any strong relationship, so you glorify God just by being with Him. That can be during quiet times such as prayer and meditation, but truly we can be with God at any time by simply being aware of His presence and communing with Him. Then we acknowledge and exemplify His person and presence.

We glorify God when we love Him.

Love is God's primary attribute, and He wants your love in return. Loving God brings glory to Him. By loving God, you acknowledge and exemplify His person and presence.

To restate, any time we take an action that acknowledges, proclaims, and exemplifies God's person, presence, and power, we glorify God by honoring His name as holy.

Then There's the Opposite

Sometimes we best understand a concept by examining what it doesn't mean. Misusing God's name is the opposite of honoring His name. The third of the Ten Commandments says, "Do not misuse the name of the Lord your God, because the Lord will punish anyone who misuses His name" (Exodus 20:7).

There are many ways to misuse God's name. One way is to use God's name in a curse, and another is to use His name flippantly. Voicing the name of God without regard for who He is brings dishonor.

Another way of misusing God's name is to be known as His child but act in a way that dishonors Him. Any parent can understand how God must feel when His children disobey Him, ignore His commands, or act in any other way that shows disregard for Him.

I was a pretty good student in school as I was growing up. I didn't get into much trouble and made good grades, so my parents were usually pleased with my behavior. (Let's pretend that those fights with my brothers never happened.)

I can remember how proud my parents were when I won an academic award in high school. I can also remember how upset they were when I disobeyed them. But their greatest disappointment came when I performed my misdeeds in public and dishonored the family name. One time I yelled an ugly comment to a neighbor who was driving by, and when the story got around to my parents (good news travels fast!), I experienced some pretty severe punishment, both verbally and physically.

What I didn't understand at the time was that my inappropriate behavior reflected on everyone in the family, especially my parents, and they weren't about to tolerate it. I was misusing the name I had been given.

An Example from Ancient Israel

Similarly, God wants and expects His children to live in a way that honors and glorifies Him. He made this point clear to the children of Israel on multiple occasions. "You are to be holy to Me because I, the Lord, am holy, and I have set you apart from the nations to be Mine" (Leviticus 20:26).

Unfortunately, Israel repeatedly rebelled against God throughout its history. God continually warned the Israelites to repent of their sins and honor Him, but over the years they went from bad to worse. Second Kings 17:7–20 contains a long list of God's grievances against Israel, eventually resulting in their downfall.

When the Lord tore Israel from the house of David, Israel made Jeroboam son of Nebat king. Then Jeroboam led Israel away from following the Lord and caused them to commit great sin. The Israelites persisted in all the sins that Jeroboam committed and did not turn away from them. Finally, the Lord removed Israel from His presence just as He had declared through all His servants the prophets. So Israel has been exiled to Assyria from their homeland until today. (2 Kings 17:21–23)

Because of His great mercy, God delayed this punishment for several hundred years. He sent many prophets to proclaim His message so the Israelites would turn back to Him, but it was to no avail. Their refusal to honor the One who had provided them a land and a promise eventually spelled their doom. The southern kingdom of Judah still remained, but they eventually met the same end for the same reason.

God is serious that those who take His name are to honor Him, and that includes us. Christians must live in a way to honor the name we have taken. Christ is holy, so we are to be holy, and we are to honor the name of Christ as holy. "As obedient children, do not be conformed to the desires of your former ignorance but, as the One who called you is holy, you also are to be holy in all your conduct; for it is written, 'Be holy, because I am holy'" (1 Peter 1:14–16).

Though our circumstances differ from ancient Israel's, the principle is the same. Israel was God's chosen nation through whom He would bless all nations. As Christians, we are to take God's message of salvation in Christ to all people.

The Israelites received God's laws through Moses and were accountable to obey them; we have received the commands of Christ and are equally liable to fulfill them.

Israel as a nation ultimately paid the price for dishonoring God. Though we have the sure promise of salvation, we also experience consequences when we dishonor our Father.

The bottom line is that God is holy and deserves honor, so our primary responsibility is to glorify God in our thoughts, words, and deeds.

God vs. Ego

There is a subtle but dangerous issue here. We in America like to think that we can live independently, capitalizing on our own ability and native intelligence to forge the kind of life we desire for ourselves. We want to be the captain of our own ship.

Many Christians take this approach to life, but you won't find it endorsed in the Bible. Ultimately, you must either glorify God or glorify yourself. Most people don't want to give up the attention, credit, and respect that God deserves because that's what they want for themselves. But God must receive them. You must deny yourself, as Jesus said in Luke 9:23: "If anyone wants to come with Me, he must deny himself, take up his cross daily, and follow Me."

So you must constantly make a choice: will you glorify yourself or will you glorify God? If you are going to be the person God wants you to be, you must choose self-denial, not self-reliance.

Living this way is diametrically opposed to the American ideal of rugged individualism and independence. It's tough for us westerners to handle because it demands full dependence on God and rejection of self. This kind of life takes real discipline, but it is the key to living the Christian life. We will frequently discover that the result is truly worth the sacrifice. As Jesus said, "For whoever wants to save his life will lose it, but whoever loses his life because of Me will save it. What is a man benefited if he gains the whole world, yet loses or forfeits himself?" (Luke 9:24–25).

God Has a Purpose for Your Life

What are you living for? For what or whom would you die? What are you trying to accomplish in life? In what way do you want people to remember you? What do you stand for? These questions are at their heart asking the same thing: what is your purpose in life?

Most people I know have set goals for themselves and have a general idea of what they should be doing. But the great majority of them have never really identified what their life's purpose is or should be. On the numerous occasions when I have directly asked a person about their purpose in life, only rarely have I received anything close to a real answer. Most people say something about what brings them happiness or what short-term goals they have. My conclusion is that most people have never seriously considered their purpose in life.

In contrast, God has a purpose for everything He has created: "The Lord has prepared everything for His purpose—even the wicked for the day of disaster" (Proverbs 16:4).

He has designed us to honor His name as holy, that is, to bring glory to Him and Him alone. That is God's overall purpose for each person's life. "Therefore, whether you eat or drink, or whatever you do, do everything for God's glory" (1 Corinthians 10:31). "In Him we were also made His inheritance, predestined according to the purpose of the One who works out everything in agreement with the decision of His will, so that we who had already put our hope in the Messiah might bring praise to His glory. In Him you also, when you heard the word of truth, the gospel of your salvation—in Him when you believed—were sealed with the promised Holy Spirit. He is the down payment of our inheritance, for the redemption of the possession, to the praise of His glory" (Ephesians 1:11–14).

Even when people live in a way that opposes God, they will ultimately glorify and praise Him. Quoting Isaiah 45:23, Paul said, "For it is written: 'As I live, says the Lord, every knee will bow to Me, and every tongue will give praise to God.' So then, each of us will give an account of himself to God" (Romans 14:11–12).

Ezekiel pointed out that God would restore Israel from exile, not because they deserved it, but to honor His holy name: "Therefore, say to the house of Israel: This is what the Lord God says: It is not for your sake that I will act, house of Israel, but for My holy name, which you profaned among the nations where you went. I will honor the holiness of My great name, which has been profaned among the nations—the name you have profaned among them. The nations will know that I am Yahweh"—the declaration of the Lord God—"when I demonstrate My holiness through you in their sight" (Ezekiel 36:22–23).

We've already seen that because God is the source of all that exists, He is worthy of all honor and praise, and His glory is the ultimate purpose for everything that exists. Therefore, your purpose in life is also to bring glory to God. So by praying, "Your name be honored as holy," you are praying that God's true purpose would be accomplished in your life, and that you are seeking to live the kind of life that truly honors God. Instead of seeking for your name to be glorified, you are seeking glory for His name.

The main point of this chapter is that God's purpose for your life is to glorify Him. By living for your true purpose, you will be happiest and most fulfilled. You settle for less when you live life on your own terms, for your own purposes and goals.

Praying to Honor God's Name

Now that we've examined the phrase "Your name be honored as holy" in detail, let's see how that translates into actual prayer. There are three obvious areas to consider.

First, simply praise God and honor Him for who He is. He is the one who is worthy of all glory. The entire universe praises Him, so join in that chorus to declare God's supreme worthiness. Most of us spend too little time praising God through prayer. A good place to start is to read one of the many Psalms that praise God and then meditate on it, adding your own thoughts of praise. You can also think of a song of praise and either sing it out loud or just read it, with God as your audience. Let the Holy Spirit guide you into creative ways of glorifying God in prayer.

Secondly, since God's purpose for your life is to glorify Him, you can pray for yourself. When you realize that God is perfect, infinite, and holy, it's natural to pray that your life will reflect that. Specifically, pray that:

» your life's purpose will truly be to honor God's name as holy

» you will seek God's glory ahead of your own

» all your thoughts and actions will bring honor to God

And you can pray for others. As previously noted, all creation glorifies God because He mandated it. The only exception is mankind. Because God granted us the ability to think and choose freely, we have the option to dishonor God, and we frequently take that option. By praying that other people will glorify God in their lives, you are asking for God's highest purpose to be achieved, and that prayer honors God.

You can pray for God's purpose in the lives of many individuals, including family members, friends, and fellow church members. You can also pray for missionaries, government officials, military personnel, and persecuted Christians, among others. One of the exercises at the end of the chapter is designed to help you identify people to pray for in this way.

Remember Your Purpose

It's always a good idea to remember the purpose of what we're doing so that we don't lose perspective and act in a way contrary to that purpose. As our children were growing, I spent a good amount of time coaching their sports teams. I eventually got into umpiring Little League softball and baseball, and that was a real learning experience.

The great majority of players, coaches, parents, and other spectators understand the real purpose of children's sports. But most of us have witnessed the behavior of someone who has forgotten that purpose, like a coach who somehow believes his team is playing in the World Series, a parent who thinks her daughter is the next Dot Richardson, or a player who flaunts bad sportsmanship so that no one really wants to be around him.

These people are focused on their own selfish ends and have lost sight of the game's true purpose. It isn't to win at all costs, trample on the other team, or belittle a player to boost one's own self-worth. Or, as I experienced too often, to ridicule an umpire's call, question his integrity, or blame the game's outcome on his decision. The purpose is to enjoy the game, develop teamwork and skills, and build character. But you'd never know it by watching the behavior at some games!

Life is like that. Some people are out to get whatever they can for themselves in this life. When the chips are down, they look out for No. 1. Their overall purpose is to be able to shout, "I got mine!"

Jesus said that we should do the opposite. In essence, your approach to life should be completely selfless. You are to give up your own self-interest, selfishness, and self-centeredness. Your life's purpose must be to bring glory to God, not to yourself. He said it this way: "You are the light of the world. A city situated on a hill cannot be hidden. No one lights a lamp and puts it under a basket, but rather on a lampstand, and it gives light for all who are in the house. In the same way, let your light shine before men, so that they may see your good works and give glory to your Father in heaven" (Matthew 5:14–16).

Since God has made you perfect*, you have a perfect motive to glorify Him. You can live in such a way that others, on seeing your life, will give glory to God. Then you will achieve God's ultimate purpose for your life. That's why you are to pray, "Your name be honored as holy."

Chapter Summary

- » Honoring God's name as holy is the first and most important part of our prayer.
- » We are called Christians, so we must live in a way to honor the name we have taken.
- » God has an overall purpose for your life: to honor His name as holy.
- » You should pray that God's purpose will be accomplished in your life and the lives of other people.
- » Main point: Your principal purpose in life is to glorify God by honoring His name as holy.

Pursuing Perfect* Passion

For personal or group study

1. What is it about God's name that warrants honor and glory?

2. What is praise? In your opinion, why is praising God so important? How do you praise God? How can your life lead others to praise God?

3. David praised God in prayer in 1 Chronicles 29:10–13. What was the occasion for this prayer? For what specific things did David praise God? How does this prayer help you to praise God in your prayers?

4. Glorifying God means to acknowledge, proclaim, and exemplify God's person, presence, and power. Combining each of these verbs with each of the three nouns yields nine different ways to glorify God (for example, acknowledging His presence; proclaiming His power). Describe a specific example of honoring God each of these nine ways.

5. Read Psalm 8:1–2; Matthew 2:2, 5:16, 21:12–16; and Romans 12:2. Then, for each passage, pray for God's insight and write responses to these questions:

   » How do these verses show that God's purpose for you is to glorify Him?

   » In what specific ways will you live to glorify God?

6. Imagine that you've somehow learned that you have only one more month to live. How has your life glorified God to this point? What has been the purpose of your life? What will you do over the next thirty days? How will that bring purpose and meaning to your life?

7. For whom can you pray God's purpose for their life? List specific people in each of these areas:
    » Family: immediate, extended
    » Friends: neighborhood, work, school
    » Church: leaders, members
    » Public: government, military, sports, entertainment
    » Other individuals and groups

8. As a Christian, the Spirit of Christ abides in you (see Romans 8:9–11). What can you do to live so that people see Jesus reflected in your life?

6

God's Kingdom: Your Priority

Your kingdom come.
—Matthew 6:10

There are various types of governments in the world today. Most countries enjoy the benefits of a constitution that provides for a president, congress, parliament, or some other set of leaders to maintain continuity of governmental affairs. Although individuals and parties can still cause problems, these forms of government tend toward stability.

Few kingdoms remain where the ruling monarch wields absolute authority. Over time, as democracy has grown and spread, people have been less and less willing to submit to a single autocratic ruler. Some of the remaining kingdoms are now experiencing turmoil as people rebel against a repressive regime. Perhaps one day there will be no more kings who govern with complete dominion.

In contrast, during biblical times, most nations were ruled by a king. The ruling power in Jesus' time was the Roman Empire, and the Jews were well aware of the authority wielded by the emperor.

Local authorities such as Pontius Pilate and Herod Antipas aggressively executed that authority. Roman soldiers were always about, ready to put down any kind of uprising. Tax collectors continually extracted denarii for Rome as well as their own exorbitant fees. Anyone daring to defy Roman rule was quickly and harshly dispatched. Life under an earthly king was at once both stable and uncertain.

So when Jesus said "Your kingdom come," His listeners had no trouble relating to the idea of a king. The real question in their minds was most likely related to the nature of that kingdom.

What is God's Kingdom?

For a kingdom to exist there must be a king, and there must be subjects who submit to the king's rule and jurisdiction. So if you are in God's kingdom, He must reign over your heart and mind. That's what God's kingdom is: His rule over your life and the lives of all other citizens of His kingdom. He's the king, and those people who have trusted Jesus for salvation are His subjects.

Jesus taught about the kingdom in parables, partially because He wanted to make a difficult concept understandable to our limited minds. Here are a few of the many parables that Jesus told about God's kingdom:

> » From the parable of the sower, we learn that everyone who wants to enter the kingdom must be receptive to God's word.

> » From the parable of the weeds, we learn that some people who pretend to be in the kingdom are really counterfeit Christians.

> » From the parable of the mustard seed, we learn that the kingdom will inevitably grow from a small start to the size God intends.

> » From the parable of the hidden treasure and the parable of the pearl, we learn that entry into the kingdom is so valuable that it is worth sacrificing everything else we have.

> »   From the parable of the unmerciful servant, we learn that forgiveness is expected from kingdom citizens.

> »   From the parable of the ten virgins, we learn to be vigilant for the fulfillment of the kingdom.

Although He instituted it here on earth among human beings, God's kingdom is not an earthly one. Jesus made it clear to Pilate that His kingdom is a spiritual dominion that is totally unlike earthly kingdoms: "'My kingdom is not of this world,' said Jesus. 'If My kingdom were of this world, My servants would fight, so that I wouldn't be handed over to the Jews. As it is, My kingdom does not have its origin here'" (John 18:36).

Who is in God's Kingdom?

There are many religions in the world today and many people following them. Most of these people are trying to earn their way to heaven, score enough points to be worthy of God's kingdom, or even become gods themselves at some point. They are hoping to achieve their goal by taking whatever their religion says as the proper path.

By the world's standards, some of them are very good people. They contribute to society. They help a lot of people. They do a lot of good things. Of course, some of them do some pretty bad things, too, but that's beside the point. The point is that they are religious people.

Unfortunately for them, all these religious people ignore the truth that God is the only one who can make you perfect* enough to be worthy of heaven. That's the difference between Christianity and all the world's religions. Religions are built around human beings praying enough prayers, performing enough rituals, doing enough good works, making pilgrimages to enough holy places, or whatever else is required to earn your way to heaven. The problem with the religious approach is that God will not allow an imperfect creature into His perfect heaven. No matter what anyone does, they will never be perfect enough to warrant a place in God's kingdom.

Christianity is different because it isn't really about religion. Instead, it's about a relationship with God through Jesus Christ. He restores the relationship that we broke by our own sin. We've already seen that God makes us perfect* through His effort, not ours. To enter God's kingdom (and thus be worthy of entering heaven after this life), we must depend on God through faith in Jesus. We then have intimacy with God both here and hereafter.

God's kingdom consists of those people who have consciously entered His kingdom. They have willfully submitted themselves to His rule. No one simply wakes up one day and realizes, "Oh, wow, I'm in God's kingdom!" It doesn't happen that way. Instead, God's kingdom citizens are those who have accepted the new life that He freely offers by grace through faith in Jesus Christ. The Holy Spirit has moved them to become God's subjects.

Why is God's Kingdom Important?

All kingdoms, organizations, and institutions will eventually fail and cease to exist. Except God's kingdom. It is the only permanent institution there will ever be. It alone will survive forever. That's why the growth and prosperity of God's kingdom are important.

Of course, that's one of the greatest benefits of being a kingdom subject. We will have eternal life in heaven, living forever in God's presence. As the saying goes, it just doesn't get any better than that.

And since it's God's desire to have that eternal relationship with every person, we should help other people understand God's kingdom so that they can also become kingdom citizens. Then they too can have eternal intimacy with the One who created them.

Just How Does God's Kingdom Come?

Now that we have a grasp of the meaning and value of God's kingdom, what does it mean for it to come? There are three verb tenses to examine: past, future, and present.

God's kingdom *did come* at Pentecost.

When Jesus was about to return to heaven forty days after His resurrection, He gave the disciples a clue about the coming events.

> While He was together with them, He commanded them not to leave Jerusalem, but to wait for the Father's promise. "This," He said, "is what you heard from Me; for John baptized with water, but you will be baptized with the Holy Spirit not many days from now." So when they had come together, they asked Him, "Lord, at this time are You restoring the kingdom to Israel?" He said to them, "It is not for you to know times or periods that the Father has set by His own authority. But you will receive power when the Holy Spirit has come upon you, and you will be My witnesses in Jerusalem, in all Judea and Samaria, and to the ends of the earth." (Acts 1:4–8)

Even though His disciples still didn't understand His kingdom, they were about to experience it firsthand. Sure enough, on the day of Pentecost, the Holy Spirit came to them with great power, Peter preached a remarkable sermon, and three thousand people became citizens of God's kingdom.

God's kingdom *will come* at the final judgment.

When God draws the world and time to an end, His kingdom will be finally consummated. It was revealed to John this way: "The seventh angel blew his trumpet, and there were loud voices in heaven saying: The kingdom of the world has become the kingdom of our Lord and of His Messiah, and He will reign forever and ever!" (Revelation 11:15).

The physical world that we know will be no more, and the people in God's kingdom will become immortal. "Brothers, I tell you this: flesh and blood cannot inherit the kingdom of God, and corruption cannot inherit incorruption. Listen! I am telling you a mystery: We will not all fall asleep, but we will all be changed, in a moment, in the twinkling of an eye, at the last trumpet. For the trumpet will sound, and the dead will be raised incorruptible, and we will be changed. Because this corruptible must be clothed with incorruptibility, and this mortal must be clothed with immortality" (1 Corinthians 15:50–53).

God's kingdom *comes now* as it continues to grow on earth.
Until God brings history to a close, His kingdom will continue to grow and prosper on earth. It grows when a new citizen enters the kingdom. Each time someone becomes a Christian, that's one more member of God's family. He desires for His kingdom to grow as each individual enters a love relationship with Him.

The kingdom also comes when its citizens yield their lives to God's rule and reign because that strengthens the kingdom. No king wants weak, ineffective subjects. How can He fight the battles to be waged with a feeble army?

Each of us should strive to become model citizens so that God's kingdom will be stronger and more vibrant. God's kingdom comes when its citizens become so much like Jesus that the whole world is polarized into those who are drawn to us and those who abhor us—just like with Jesus. Jesus' presence in the world causes people to show themselves for who they really are: children of God or children of Satan.

Finally, God's kingdom comes when its citizens act as ambassadors. By passing along the good news that everyone can apply for citizenship, we assist God as He builds His kingdom one citizen at a time.

The Kingdom at War

Earthly kingdoms frequently engage in battle. They wage war to subdue adversarial kingdoms and take over their land, assuming they are victorious. On any given day there are dozens of battles being fought across the face of the earth.

God's kingdom is also engaged in battle. Though fought on earth, it is a spiritual struggle. The battlefield isn't on the land, sea, or sky but in the human heart. The weapon isn't a sword or a gun but prayer. Paul said that the battle isn't against the people and kingdoms of this world but against spiritual forces: "Finally, be strengthened by the Lord and by His vast strength. Put on the full armor of God so that you can stand against the tactics of the Devil. For our battle is not against flesh and blood, but against the rulers, against the authorities, against the world powers of this darkness, against the spiritual forces of evil in the heavens" (Ephesians 6:10–12).

Sure enough, Jesus joined the battle, leading His followers directly into the pivotal fray in the garden of Gethsemane. And He won decisively—on His knees! Even though Satan thought he had the upper hand, Jesus completely submitted His will to His Father's desire, and the rest is history.

It's still the same. People aren't the enemy; they are the battlefield. Satan is the enemy. The battle for the hearts of our family members, friends, and neighbors isn't waged anywhere but on our knees. Rather than taking up swords and following Jesus into battle against Roman soldiers, corrupt priests, or any other human agents, the victory is won when you deny yourself, take up your cross, and follow Him.

Your Life's Priority

Soon after saying the Model Prayer, Jesus addressed the issue of priorities. His main point was that people usually put their focus on things that don't matter when their chief priority should be God's kingdom: "So don't worry, saying, 'What will we eat?' or 'What will we drink?' or 'What will we wear?' For the idolaters eagerly seek all these things, and your heavenly Father knows that you need them. But seek first the kingdom of God and His righteousness, and all these things will be provided for you" (Matthew 6:31–33).

What is a priority? Stemming from the word "prior," a priority is something that comes before anything else. Your top priority is whatever comes first when you utilize your resources. For example, if your top priority is entertainment, you'll spend your time and energy watching TV, playing computer games, and going to sports events, plays, and movies. You'll spend your money on the latest electronic equipment, a bigger TV, and season football tickets. Entertainment is just one example. Other priorities can be work, power, money, or pleasure.

But what if God's kingdom is your top priority? Then you'll spend your time, money, and energy first on God's kingdom and righteousness. Your thoughts will first go to submitting to God's rule in your life. Your time will first go to prayer, Bible study, and worship. Your money will first go to tithing and supporting missions. Your energy will first go to those ministries to which God is calling you. God's kingdom must be first in your life: the first thing in the morning, the first appointment on your schedule, the first task to accomplish, the first thought on your mind, the first words on your lips, the first place in your heart.

God's kingdom must take precedence over everything else that vies for your attention. You must seek God's rule and reign in your heart and mind. You must work with God on the assignments that He gives you as He builds His kingdom. You must seek to invite others into God's kingdom.

In the previous chapter, we discussed the difference between glorifying God and glorifying self. Similarly, to be useful to God's kingdom, you need to forgo building your own kingdom. That is, you must give up the right to rule in your own life. You don't have the prerogative to balance God's priorities with your own priorities; God's priorities must always take first place. You must sacrifice your own desires so that God's kingdom is always your top priority. Again, that requires self-denial and discipline, but the result is always worth the sacrifice.

Jesus said that when you put God's kingdom first "all these things will be provided for you" (Matthew 6:33). He was saying that you don't need to worry about the things other people think are priorities because God will supply all your needs. After all, "Your heavenly Father knows that you need them."

We'll take up this subject in more detail in a later chapter. For now, the key point is that when you really trust God to provide what you need, it's a lot easier to put His kingdom first because you know He's got your back.

Genuinely praying "Your kingdom come" demands total commitment on your part because it is equivalent to making God's kingdom your top priority. When you do that, God enables you to line up all the remaining priorities in the proper order. He will also guide you to give up those things that shouldn't have any priority in your life, whether or not you think they belong. And as we will see in the next chapter, putting the kingdom first enables you to do God's will on a daily basis.

A Model Kingdom Citizen

God wants model citizens in His kingdom. A model citizen of a city obeys its laws and promotes its welfare. She volunteers her time to help others and puts the city's interests above her own. A model citizen is universally admired because she makes the city better and stronger.

In the same way, a model citizen of God's kingdom is one who helps the kingdom grow and prosper. He trusts and depends on God, obeys His commands, and loves his neighbor as himself. A model citizen acts as an ambassador to invite others into God's kingdom: "Therefore, we are ambassadors for Christ; certain that God is appealing through us, we plead on Christ's behalf, 'Be reconciled to God'" (2 Corinthians 5:20).

God has chosen to do His kingdom work through us in evangelism, missions, prayer, and ministry because He loves us. A good parent teaches his children to do chores because he loves them and knows they'll eventually have to do their own work. Similarly, God wants us to work with Him to build His kingdom.

When we do everything the way that God wants, then He can use us to the greatest effectiveness and His kingdom prospers. When we are rebellious, lazy, or indifferent, He has to look elsewhere for the people He can work through.

Don't miss the opportunity to be a model citizen for God's kingdom in this life. Make His kingdom your top priority. Pray that it comes in your life and the lives of others.

Praying for God's Kingdom to Come

When Jesus said to pray "Your kingdom come," He could have meant to pray for the kingdom's initiation at Pentecost. That prayer was answered two millennia ago.

To pray that God's kingdom will be fulfilled at the end of time is praying for the inevitable. God has a timetable for that to happen, but He has decided not to share the details (though that doesn't stop some people from trying to figure it all out). I can ask God to consummate His kingdom on my schedule, but I seriously doubt that He'll change His mind.

That leaves the current "coming" of God's kingdom, and Jesus simply said to pray that it comes. Here are some ways we can do that:

» If you aren't already in God's kingdom, you can ask Him to make you a citizen (i.e., pray for salvation through faith in Christ).

» Pray that His kingdom becomes and remains your highest priority.

» Pray that you will be a model citizen in the kingdom.

» Pray that more people become citizens of the kingdom.

» Pray by name for each person who you know who does not have a relationship with God to turn to Him for salvation.

» Pray that all kingdom citizens become model citizens.

Chapter Summary

- » God's kingdom consists of His rule and reign in the hearts and minds of His people.

- » God's kingdom came at Pentecost; it continues to come as God builds it; and it will be fulfilled at the final judgment.

- » You can pray for God's kingdom to come, grow, and prosper in your life and the lives of others.

- » Your life's priority is to seek God's kingdom by being a model kingdom citizen and acting as an ambassador to invite others in.

- » Main point: Seeking and living in God's kingdom is to be your top priority in life.

Pursuing Perfect* Passion

1. How well can you relate to the idea of a kingdom? What about your citizenship in God's kingdom appeals to you? What parts of the concept trouble you?

2. Read several parables about God's kingdom and write the principle that you think Jesus was trying to teach. Here are some in addition to those listed in the chapter:

   » The vineyard (Mark 12:1–9)

   » The yeast (Matthew 13:33)

   » The rich man and Lazarus (Luke 16:19–31)

   » The vineyard workers (Matthew 20:1–16)

3. Explain in your own words the tension between God's kingdom being a spiritual kingdom while growing in an earthly setting.

4. How often do you pray for the growth of God's kingdom? What are the specifics of those prayers?

5. How well do you relate to the idea that you are engaged in warfare when you pray for God's kingdom? Do you consider yourself to be a "prayer warrior"? How does the idea of spiritual warfare help us as kingdom citizens?

6. What are your current life priorities? How often do you consider your priorities? What do you do to manage them?

7. Do you think that it's reasonable for Jesus to ask you to make His kingdom your top priority? Why or why not? Are there other priorities in your life that you feel should be just as important as or more important than God's kingdom?

8. For God's kingdom to become your top priority, what changes would you have to make? On which habits, pastimes, or relationships would you need to place less emphasis? More emphasis? Do you consider it worthwhile to make those changes? Why or why not?

9. From a practical standpoint, what can you do to become more like a model citizen of God's kingdom? Are you willing to do that?

10. Imagine what your life would be like if you were an ambassador to another country. Does that idea appeal to you? Why or why not? How does your attitude affect your role as an ambassador for God's kingdom?

7

GOD'S WILL: YOUR PRACTICE

Your will be done on earth as it is in heaven.
—Matthew 6:10

SEVERAL YEARS AGO MY FRIEND Richard decided to retire. After twenty-six years of owning and operating his own company, he sold it to his employees. Most people who knew him wondered why a man in his forties with a successful business would simply drop it all, but Richard was confident that God was guiding him to do just that.

"When people ask me what I'm going to do," he said, "I tell them that I don't know. First thing every day when I get up, I pray and listen for God's direction, and whatever He tells me to do, I do it."

I remarked that daily listening for God's will and obeying it must be an exciting way to live. After all, that seems to be the way Jesus lived, and we certainly want to be like Him. "Yes," Richard replied, "but the hard part is making sure that you are really hearing what God is saying."

That's so true. We know that God speaks to us through various means, such as the Bible, prayer, and even life's events. But how do we know specifically what God is saying? What is His will for any given situation? How do we know what to do today?

What Does Jesus Mean?

Before we try to answer those questions, let's look carefully at Jesus' words: "Your will be done on earth as it is in heaven." Two points stand out.

We are to pray that God's will is done on earth.
What is God's will? Simply, it is His desire in any and all circumstances. Being perfect, He has a perfect will that is ideal for every person and every event in every situation. Doing God's will is doing what Jesus would do in the same situation because Jesus always did God's will. We are to pray for God's will, not our own or someone else's.

We are to pray that God's will is done on earth *as it is in heaven.*
We've seen that heaven is God's perfect dwelling, so undoubtedly His will is done throughout heaven, completely and perfectly. For His will to be done that way on earth means the same: completely and perfectly.

God's Global Will

It seems that if God's will were done perfectly on earth, we would have heaven right here. There would be no poverty, war, or famine. We'd all be happy and fulfilled, spending our days glorifying God and enjoying His presence.

That's not the case because much of what happens in the world isn't God's will. Every time someone sins, that's not God's will. When people or nations choose to act based on selfish, dishonest, or cruel motives, that's not God's will. Children starve, armies battle, dictators oppress, criminals steal, and leaders lie every day. God doesn't want it that way because the Earth becomes less like heaven every time His will isn't done.

Though it may seem like a losing proposition to pray for God's will in a world that is so driven by evil, we need to remember that God is bigger than all of these things. What is outside our control isn't too difficult for Him. As He said to Moses, "Is the Lord's power limited? You will see whether or not what I have promised will happen to you" (Numbers 11:23).

So our prayer must be for God's will to be done across our communities, nation, and world. We can pray for conflicts to be resolved, people to be healed, and justice to be carried out. We are to ask God to work in the physical, emotional, financial, social, mental, and spiritual aspects of people's lives. There are absolutely no limits when it comes to praying for God's will to be done on earth as it is in heaven.

God's Unique Will for You

Now back to your life. What about those things over which you have some control? Doesn't God have a unique, specific will for you as an individual? Yes, He does. We observed in Chapter 5 that God's purpose for each person is to glorify Him, but He also has specific, unique purposes for specific, unique people. Here are some biblical examples:

» God used Moses to lead His people out of slavery and establish His laws (see Exodus 3:10).

» God used Cyrus to set His people free, rebuild Jerusalem, and make His name known (see Isaiah 44:24–45:13).

» Jesus healed the man born blind so that God's work would be evident (see John 9:3).

» God used the apostle Paul to spread the gospel across the Mediterranean world (see Acts 9:15, 26:15–18).

When people talk about doing God's will, that's usually what they have in mind. They want to know God's specific plan for them at specific points in their life, and the Bible is clear that God has those specifics in mind. He has assignments that are unique to your life and your situation. If you don't perform them, they may not get done.

He may bring someone across your path who needs to know Christ's love. If you don't take the opportunity, that person may not get the message. Or God may want to turn your life in another direction because He wants to build His kingdom through you. If you aren't listening for His voice, that work may not get done, and you may not experience the blessings He has for you.

Several years ago, God called me to be a church pastor. Fortunately, I had sensed that He had something in mind for me to do, and I was actively seeking to understand what that might involve. When the specifics of His call became clear, it was an easy decision. God enabled me to pastor a church for five years while I kept my secular job. He worked through that church and blessed me and others as we continued to seek His will. For you, and for God's kingdom, it's important to understand God's will and do it.

How Can You Know?

To repeat the previous questions:

» How do you know what God is saying to you specifically?

» What is His will for any given situation?

» How do you know what to do today?

One answer is that you must remain close enough to God that you can actually hear His voice. You can't hold a conversation with someone out of earshot. And even if the person is sitting just a few feet away, you sometimes still can't be heard. (Parents of teenagers will know what I mean.) God sometimes has trouble getting through to us because either we are far away from Him or we just aren't listening. So we need to remain close and attentive. Intimacy with God helps open your ears. That comes from daily Bible reading, prayer, meditation, and worship.

Even when we are close to God, it isn't always easy to discern God's will. Sometimes we don't seem to hear anything when we ask. Even when we do get the message, we aren't always certain whether it's God,

Satan, or self that is speaking. Some people have claimed to be doing God's will even when committing atrocities such as murder. Christians sometimes believe that a particular action is God's will simply because the circumstances seem to point that way, only later to discover that they were on the wrong track entirely.

So how do we distinguish God's voice from our own? How do we know when we are being influenced by Satan and the world? God doesn't normally write His messages on the wall or across the sky, so we need to be able to discern God's will from competing messages. In *Experiencing God*, Henry Blackaby and Claude King point out that there are four basic ways that God speaks through the Holy Spirit to help us understand His will: the Bible, prayer, circumstances, and the church.[3]

Dr. Blackaby says that if you are trying to discern God's will, you should seek to hear Him through these four means. When you see them begin to line up with the same message, then you can be confident that you are really hearing from God.

We should not trust the feeling we get from only one of these methods. A classic example is that someone may believe that they know God's will based only on recent events and circumstances, but their conclusion doesn't match what the Bible says. This approach, which is loaded with self-deception, inevitably results in pain and regret on the part of all involved. In such cases, it's vital to understand that God will not contradict Himself. You must check out all the possible ways to hear His voice. If the circumstantial evidence conflicts with what the Bible says, what you get from praying, and what you hear from solid Christian teaching, then you'd better think again.

My Way or God's Way

Once you are confident that you have heard and understood God's will, you must still decide whether you will obey it, and that's where

---

3   Henry Blackaby and Claude V. King, *Experiencing God* (Nashville: Broadman & Holman, 1994), 32.

you encounter another set of issues. The reason is that, as we've already seen, we are prone to satisfy our own selfish desires. We are sinful by nature, so doing God's will doesn't come naturally.

The world doesn't help us here because it celebrates those people who set out to blaze their own trail. The unique individual who spurns conformity and chooses his own path is considered heroic. They seem to think that the song "My Way" by Paul Anka gives good advice when it tells a man, "To say the things he truly feels, and not the words of one who kneels. The record shows I took the blows, and did it my way."

Earlier in life I mainly concentrated on doing the things I wanted to do. Essentially I asked myself, "What can I do to maximize my enjoyment in life? What is most fulfilling, satisfying, and enjoyable to me?" Then I chose to do the things that seemed most likely to make me happy.

Most people are like that. Some want constant entertainment, so they seek people and events that will entertain them. Some want to fulfill their potential. They seek activities, causes, and groups that will maximize their abilities in their chosen arena of life. Some seek pleasure: sex, drugs, money, power—whatever they think will give the most gratification of their desires. Others, known as "adrenaline junkies," look for big thrills through activities too risky for the rest of us, such as bungee jumping, sky diving, and ice climbing (um, no thanks).

No doubt about it, the world's approach is self-determination. There is no shortage of information on the subject of self. We hear a lot about "getting the most out of life." We're told to seek those things that will make us the happiest, to choose what maximizes our feeling of well-being. A lot of commercial advertising is based on self-gratification.

Once again, however, Jesus commands us to give up our own desires in favor of God's. When I began to ask God to change my perspective to match His, I heard His commands much more clearly, and I was more inclined to seek and do His will. The results began to be more favorable for me, and I could contribute to His kingdom work much more effectively. When I say to God, "Your will be done," by corollary I also have to say, "Forget my will; it no longer matters."

Your Daily Practice

Every day, many times a day, you have a choice. You can do what you want or you can do what God wants. As we've seen, it's easy to do what we want to do. Unfortunately, choosing for self is the opposite of choosing for God. "There is a way that seems right to a man, but its end is the way to death" (Proverbs 14:12).

To do the will of God, we must exercise discipline, which means to consciously choose the right thing to do, and that's not easy. To pray "Your will be done," you must shift from a focus on self to a focus on God. The Bible has plenty to say about that, too:

» "Trust in the Lord with all your heart, and do not rely on your own understanding; think about Him in all your ways, and He will guide you on the right paths" (Proverbs 3:5–6).

» "But seek first the kingdom of God and His righteousness, and all these things will be provided for you" (Matthew 6:33).

» "Then Jesus said to His disciples, 'If anyone wants to come with Me, he must deny himself, take up his cross, and follow Me. For whoever wants to save his life will lose it, but whoever loses his life because of Me will find it. What will it benefit a man if he gains the whole world yet loses his life? Or what will a man give in exchange for his life?'" (Matthew 16:24–26).

Doing what God wants should become your daily practice. It is the option you should always choose. You must do God's will in all your actions on earth, and you are to do it fully, perfectly, and completely, as it is in heaven.

This approach is consistent with the other parts of the Model Prayer. If you want to honor God's name as holy, you will choose to do what pleases Him. When you make God's kingdom your top priority, you take actions that are consistent with His kingdom work. The perfect* result is that you do God's will more and more as you seek to hear and obey it as a daily practice.

Naturally, you won't be perfect at it. You will still choose self some of the time, just like everyone else, and that is the essence of sin. Nevertheless, your daily practice should be to perform God's will. Just like a physician practices medicine and an attorney practices law, you are to practice the will of God.

It would be wonderful if doctors and lawyers never erred, always prescribing the best treatment and giving the best advice, but they aren't perfect either. Fortunately, they can get better with practice. Over time, with practice, you too will get better at hearing and obeying God's voice.

There are many biblical examples of people who chose to practice God's will. Joseph chose to obey God's commands to serve as Jesus' earthly father (see Matthew 1:18–2:23). He apparently didn't live to see Jesus begin His ministry, but he was perhaps the most important earthly father who ever lived. John chose to herald the coming of his cousin Jesus and baptize Him (see Matthew 3:1–17), but his practice of God's will cost him his head—literally. Jesus chose to obey His Father when tempted otherwise (see Matthew 4:1–11), and we know the end of that story.

The point of these examples is that doing God's will always brings fulfillment and joy, but it will also be accompanied by sacrifice. The way of self, Satan, and the world may seem attractive, and it's usually a lot easier in the short run, but the end result is never good and always includes problems for us and others. Jesus told us to "hunger and thirst for righteousness" (Matthew 5:6). He also said, "My food is to do the will of Him who sent Me and to finish His work" (John 4:34). Our passion for the will of God should be the same. Without food and water we soon die. Our lives should depend just as much on doing God's will.

Obstacles

Once we hear God's instructions, it takes discipline to act on them, but there are still some obstacles to overcome. Defiance and desire frequently get in the way.

Obedience vs. Defiance

King Saul learned firsthand the difference between obedience and defiance. God had directed Saul to destroy the sinful Amalekites. Saul led the army to defeat them, but instead of destroying everything as God had said, they kept the best of the plunder. God's response was immediate: "Then the word of the Lord came to Samuel: 'I regret that I made Saul king, for he has turned away from following Me and has not carried out My instructions'" (1 Samuel 15:10–11).

Samuel confronted Saul and demanded to know why he had failed to obey God. Saul's defense was that he did obey and simply kept the best sheep and cattle to sacrifice to the Lord. Samuel's reply is classic: "Does the Lord take pleasure in burnt offerings and sacrifices as much as in obeying the Lord? Look: to obey is better than sacrifice, to pay attention is better than the fat of rams. For rebellion is like the sin of divination, and defiance is like wickedness and idolatry. Because you have rejected the word of the Lord, He has rejected you as king" (1 Samuel 15:22–23).

The application is obvious. We can do all kinds of things that we think are God's wishes, but what He really wants is for us to obey His words. Although there may be nothing obviously wrong with choosing our own way of serving God, we are very likely to miss God's real will.

Obedience vs. Desire

Then there is obedience vs. desire. How much do I really want to hear God? And if I hear what He's telling me to do, how obedient do I really want to be? After all, there are some things that I want to do and some things I really don't want to do.

It's like when I used to tell one of my sons to mow the yard. The grass needed it. Our neighbors appreciated it. It was good exercise. It might have even helped him later in life. (What do you mean? Of course I used that one, just like my parents did!) So why didn't it always happen? Things like video games, sports, and friends took precedence. Given a choice, he preferred to do almost anything else. I mean, mowing grass is work. And work, by definition, isn't fun. So it boiled down to a battle between obedience and desire, and what we desire is always more attractive.

The Results of Doing God's Will

We've already seen that obeying God leads to great blessings as we daily walk with Him. Knowing that you are fulfilling His purpose in your life gives great joy and hope. Keeping His kingdom as your life's priority enables you to put the rest of your life in proper perspective. And knowing that you are pleasing God by doing His will provides peace and comfort even when there is turmoil all around.

On the other hand, consider what happened to Jesus. He did God's will perfectly His entire life, and He was crucified for it. If someone were to continually do God's will today, he might not last for long; the world might, in time, do the same to him. It's possible that he would be opposed at every turn by an increasingly evil and treacherous world until it would somehow rid itself of him. Just like the world tried to rid itself of Jesus.

What we find then is that doing God's will results in being blessed by God but opposed by the world. That happened to most of the apostles, including Paul. Since they were on board with doing God's will, they found themselves on the outs with the Jewish leaders, the Roman government, and others.

Many early disciples were ostracized, persecuted, and even killed. The same thing happens in many countries today. Governments and other religious groups persecute Christians, especially church leaders, more than anyone else.

For many people, doing God's will is still no cakewalk. Even in traditionally Christian nations such as the United States, where the danger of physical persecution is remote, those Christians who are obedient to God's will are regularly ridiculed for their behavior.

The Advantage

Did Jesus have an unfair advantage? Being one with His Father, was it easier for Him to know God's will and act on it? Are we at a disadvantage because we are prone to selfishness and sin? Though it may seem so on the surface, we are also able to know and do God's will if we seek it. Paul tells us how we can have the same advantage Jesus had: "Therefore, brothers, by the mercies of God, I urge you to present your bodies as a living sacrifice, holy and pleasing to God; this is your spiritual worship. Do not be conformed to this age, but be transformed by the renewing of your mind, so that you may discern what is the good, pleasing, and perfect will of God" (Romans 12:1–2).

Paul tells us that we can discern and perform God's will if we allow God to change us by renewing our minds. That comes from self-sacrifice—we need to completely give ourselves to God. When we do that, the Spirit of Christ has complete control of our lives, renews our minds, and leads us to know and practice God's perfect will. Jesus lived in perfect unity with His heavenly Father, and because He lives in us, we can experience the same intimacy. Just as with Jesus, the Holy Spirit is our advantage. "For through the law I have died to the law, that I might live to God. I have been crucified with Christ; and I no longer live, but Christ lives in me. The life I now live in the flesh, I live by faith in the Son of God, who loved me and gave Himself for me" (Galatians 2:19–20).

My friend Richard is still retired and still daily seeking God's will. It has taken him through many ministry and missions opportunities, such as helping to start a new church. As God has used him, He has blessed him and his family. Richard would say that he still isn't perfect at it, but he continues to listen for God's will daily and do it to the best of his ability.

What about you? Are you daily praying for God's will to be done? Do you seek to hear from God about His will and then carry it out? We know that God's will is the best in any situation, for us and for others. As you seek intimacy with God, why not continually seek His will?

Praying for God's Will

Here are some prayer suggestions to help you seek and do God's will:

» As you read the newspaper, search the Internet for news, or watch the news on television, pray for God's will to be done. Ask God to direct your prayers as you pray for His will.

» Search for information about missionaries or other Christians who are assisting God in His kingdom work in other countries. Pray for them by name, asking God's will in their situations.

» Study Bible characters to learn God's unique purpose for them. Ask God to show you His unique purpose for your life.

» When facing a particular situation, seek to hear God's will through prayer, Bible study, sermons, Christian books, advice from Christian friends, and the circumstances themselves.

» Choose one of your regular activities, such as walking, engaging in a particular sport, or having discussions with friends. Silently pray to hear God's will as you participate. How well can you hear His voice? Try to improve your listening skills over time.

» Each morning, as the day is beginning, ask God to work through you to do His will throughout that day. Stop and listen until you are confident that you've heard His direction.

» Pray that God will strengthen your self-discipline to choose His will over your own and overcome the obstacles of defiance and desire.

CHAPTER SUMMARY

- » God's will is His perfect desire for every person and situation.

- » God designed you to achieve a unique purpose in life.

- » You must learn to discern God's voice so that you can know His will.

- » It takes discipline to practice God's will over your own.

- » Rather than defying God or fulfilling your own desires, obey God.

- » The results of practicing God's will include sacrifice and fulfillment.

- » Main point: Your daily practice must be to do God's will.

Pursuing Perfect* Passion

For personal or group study

1. How do you normally try to find God's will for a given situation? How confident are you that you usually know God's will?

2. Do you believe that it's realistic to pray for God's will to be done on a global basis? Explain your answer.

3. Do you believe that God has a specific purpose for your life? If so, how important is it to you that you follow His will?

4. Have you found it difficult to distinguish between the voice of God and your own thoughts? If so, what is the source of that problem?

5. Study these Bible passages and state for each one what it teaches about God's will: Mark 3:31–35, John 7:14–18, Acts 21:10–14, and Romans 8:26–28.

6. Consult the book *Experiencing God* and note the four ways that God speaks to you: through the Bible, prayer, circumstances, and the church. Which of these four ways of hearing God seems strongest in your life? Which ones do you need to use more often?

7. How difficult is it for you to obey God's will once you know it? Is "your way" getting in the way of living God's way? (Are you more likely to do what you want than what God wants?) If you are not as obedient as you should be, what steps will you take?

8. Evaluate the degree to which your daily practice is doing God's will. How much time do you devote to considering God's will? To listening for God's voice? How often do you incorporate

God's will into your plans? How often do you discard your plans in favor of God's plans?

9. In what ways have you defied God's will, even when you were sure of it? What were the results of your defiance? How different would the outcome have been if you had obeyed?

10. Have you ever done what you thought was God's will and then experienced criticism, even from other Christians? Was the problem your interpretation of God's will or other people's perception? If you had it to do over again, would you have taken a different approach?

11. When it comes to doing God's will, how much does that depend on your own discipline vs. giving up control to the Holy Spirit?

Part Three

Calling on God in Prayer

It is clear at this point that God wants us to focus on Him first in our prayers: "Your name … Your kingdom … Your will…" When you put God first in your life, including your prayer life, everything begins to line up properly.

The second half of the Model Prayer moves the focus toward us: our needs, our sins, our paths, and our weaknesses. Once we've centered our lives on God, we are in the right place to receive what He has for us. Our human nature wants our prayers to be about us anyway. But God still urges us to see ourselves in the light of His person, presence, and power. Everything should still depend on an intimate relationship with Him and what that means for our lives. It may surprise you how greatly this perspective can change your approach to this portion of your prayer.

Notice that the pronoun "us" is used throughout these verses, as opposed to "me." Jesus directed His comments to all His listeners. He encouraged us to pray as the church—God's people gathered. Although the Model Prayer should be used by each of us as a pattern for our individual prayers, we are also to pray together.

As you examine each of the four phrases in this section, consider how they can apply not only to yourself but to your family, a small group of believers such as a Sunday school class or ministry team, and even your entire church.

8

YOUR NEED: GOD'S PROVISION

Give us today our daily bread.
—Matthew 6:11

SEVERAL YEARS AGO, WHEN OUR children were still in elementary school, Mary and I began to accumulate credit card debt. Our regular monthly expenses, eating out, family vacations—it all began to add up.

We knew that a lot of American families get into this position, and Mary and I both had good salaries, so we weren't too worried about it. But as our debt soon grew to the point where we could pay only the monthly interest, our concern began to grow with it.

When we checked the numbers and realized that it would take at least five years of severe cutbacks to pay it all off, we knew we had to take action. We cut expenses and trips, augmented our income, and tried anything else we could imagine. No matter what we did, however, a year later our debt was larger than before.

During this time of growing debt and growing concern, I had a growing sense that God was calling us to do something drastic: trust

Him. I was drawn to God's message to Israel through Malachi: "'Bring the full 10 percent into the storehouse so that there may be food in My house. Test Me in this way,' says the Lord of Hosts. 'See if I will not open the floodgates of heaven and pour out a blessing for you without measure'" (Malachi 3:10).

I sensed that God was calling us to give a tithe of our income—the first 10 percent of our salaries—to His work through our church. I felt that He was promising that He would solve our debt problem if we would put Him first in this way.

When I shared this thought with Mary, she was not convinced. She didn't understand how giving *more* of our money to the church would enable us to pay off our debt. I didn't have any rational explanation of how it could work, so we hesitated.

After several more months of deepening debt, we were finally out of options. We agreed to do what God's word said and put Him to the test—but only for a while. If we didn't see any improvement after three months, we would stop tithing and try to find some other way. Our faith wasn't very strong, but we began to write the weekly checks, painful as it seemed.

After the appointed three months, amazingly enough, our debt had gone down noticeably. We weren't sure how that was happening because we weren't changing anything else, so we began to trust God a little more. We kept on tithing and within a year our credit card debt had been completely paid off. Were we relieved! God had proved Himself more than capable of providing for us. What we had failed to accomplish through our own efforts, God had somehow made happen in a miraculously short time.

That important episode taught us that there are times in life when each of us has a key question to answer: will I trust God to provide for my needs or will I devote my resources to providing them for myself? Jesus, naturally, has the correct answer to this question.

More Than Just Bread

When He used the phrase "our daily bread," Jesus wasn't just referring to the food we eat. Food is important, and for many people in today's world, it's a daily struggle just to find enough to survive. But Jesus knows that we need much more than just food and water to make it through each day. Besides food and water, most of us could quickly list many things that we need to live a full life:

- » Air to breathe
- » Physical safety and security
- » Clothing
- » Shelter
- » Emotional security
- » Meaningful relationships

For some of us, the list would be quite lengthy, which brings up the issue of needs vs. wants. Sometimes we confuse those, so let's try to clarify the issue by examining what Jesus said.

"Give us today our daily bread." It appears that Jesus was referencing Proverbs 30:8, in which the author asked for "the food I need," also translated as "my daily bread" (NIV), "food convenient for me" (KJV), or "the food allotted to me" (NKJV). Here's the whole passage, which is attributed in the first verse of the chapter to Agur son of Jakeh: "Two things I ask of You; don't deny them to me before I die: Keep falsehood and deceitful words far from me. Give me neither poverty nor wealth; feed me with the food I need. Otherwise, I might have too much and deny You, saying, 'Who is the Lord?' or I might have nothing and steal, profaning the name of my God" (Proverbs 30:7–9).

It's clear that Agur was simply asking for God to provide for his needs but no more. He asserted that either poverty or wealth would cause him to stray from God, but if God provided just what he needed, Agur would learn to depend on God daily and stay on the right path.

Jesus told us to seek that same daily dependence on God's provision for everything we need. He knows we need bread to live, but there is so much more. Our daily bread includes everything we need to do God's will, make His kingdom top priority, and glorify Him. Jesus told us to recognize that we are totally dependent on God for every part of our lives.

God, the Great Provider

God is fully aware of our needs. Being the author of life, He knows every detail of what is required for us to live and thrive, and He knows it for every individual. Furthermore, He is ready and able to provide everything we need—physically, emotionally, spiritually, financially, and socially. Once we understand all that, our natural response is complete dependence and trust. As Paul stated, "My God will supply all your needs according to His riches in glory in Christ Jesus" (Philippians 4:19).

It's important to point out that God supplies all our needs from *His* perspective. What I think I need may be significantly different from what God knows I need. God has my real needs in mind. I frequently confuse my needs with my wants. It's easy to recognize that no matter how much I may *want* a bright orange Tesla Roadster, it isn't really a crucial need in my life. But it's also easy to believe that there is some certain desire I need fulfilled in my life, even though it isn't really part of God's plan.

Jesus made this lesson clear when faced with the demand that He referee an estate settlement. Thousands of people were gathered to catch a glimpse or hear a word: "Someone from the crowd said to Him, 'Teacher, tell my brother to divide the inheritance with me.' 'Friend,' He said to him, 'who appointed Me a judge or arbitrator over you?' He then told them, 'Watch out and be on guard against all greed because one's life is not in the abundance of his possessions'" (Luke 12:13–15).

This man wanted Jesus to rectify an unjust situation where the older brother, the legal executor of his father's estate, wasn't giving his younger brother what he thought he deserved. And it may well have been a true injustice.

But Jesus chose not to address that issue. Instead, He wanted the man to see that because his focus was on money rather than on God, he was missing the real point to life. He warned him against greed and giving attention to "the abundance of his possessions." Even if he did receive all that was coming to him, he would in danger of losing what was of real value. Indeed, Jesus had just said to the crowd, "And I say to you, anyone who acknowledges Me before men, the Son of Man will also acknowledge him before the angels of God, but whoever denies Me before men will be denied before the angels of God" (Luke 12:8).

Apparently the man wasn't listening to those words but just waiting for Jesus to catch His breath so he could interrupt with his own priority. Jesus knew that he needed to turn his attention to what really mattered.

So we had better pay attention, too. Realizing that "an abundance of possessions" isn't really one of life's priorities is a difficult pill for our modern culture to swallow. We're way too absorbed with making a living out of what has nothing to do with life.

Paul is a good example here. He had a pretty cushy life when he was going around persecuting the church and enjoying the approval of the Jewish leadership. Arresting and killing Christians caused him to be feared by believers and admired by the Jews.

When God converted him on the road to Damascus, however, all that changed. From that point on he was persecuted endlessly by those same Jews, enduring arrests, beatings, imprisonment, stoning, and more. He could easily have felt that he needed a break from all these things, but instead Paul looked at it this way: "I know both how to have a little, and I know how to have a lot. In any and all circumstances I have learned the secret of being content—whether well-fed or hungry, whether in abundance or in need. I am able to do all things through Him who strengthens me" (Philippians 4:12–13).

Paul accepted whatever came from God's hand, whether it was a little or a lot, a good deal or a raw one. He knew that God has infinite resources at His disposal, so Paul didn't worry about what he actually received. He simply got along on whatever was provided. The application for us is that we must depend on God not only to supply all of our daily needs but also to determine exactly what those needs are and how He will meet them.

Notice that God provides our needs daily. He doesn't dump a lifetime's worth of resources on us all at once because He knows that we can't handle it. Instead, He provides for us as our needs occur and in His timing. Similarly, His provision is in the proper quantity, neither too little nor too much, just as Agur asked.

God is clearly interested in teaching us to trust Him, to truly believe that He can and will provide everything we need in any situation. In short, He wants us to live by faith in Him. And because of His infinite wisdom and power, God is fully capable of orchestrating our lives in this manner when we really trust Him.

Alfred E. Neuman Had It Right

When I was growing up, it was cool to read *Mad* magazine. The cover always depicted Alfred E. Neuman, a fictional character with a goofball grin, in some amusing pose designed to spoof the advertising industry, a political figure, or some other convenient target. His most famous quote was "What, me worry?" Alfred found it easy to sail through life without a single care.

Medical professionals tell us that worry is the cause of numerous physical and emotional maladies, so that's an excellent reason to stop worrying. Beyond that, there's no legitimate purpose for worry because it never produces any positive results.

Alfred had it right. Sure, there are difficult, even desperate, times in everyone's life. But worry and anxiety can never improve any situation. What we need instead is to adopt Alfred E. Neuman's perspective (well, sort of) and realize that because God is sovereign and always in charge, our best choice in any situation is to depend on Him to see us through—without worrying.

I'm not proposing that we simply skip through life oblivious to the problems and predicaments that occur, mindlessly ignoring the realities of this world. Turning a blind eye to trouble, although it never seemed to cause Alfred any harm, doesn't work in real life. It's important to recognize the people and situations that might do us harm. But we must not waste our mental and emotional resources by imagining all the potential disasters that might happen and then fretting over them. The reality is that most of the bad results we envision never happen, and in the extreme case, we can cause ourselves untold physical and emotional harm by maintaining a high level of anxiety. Instead, our response to the negative aspects of life should always be to depend on God to bring us through them.

Shortly after stating the Model Prayer, Jesus addressed the issue of worry head on. He summed it up this way: "So don't worry, saying, 'What will we eat?' or 'What will we drink?' or 'What will we wear?' For the idolaters eagerly seek all these things, and your heavenly Father knows that you need them. But seek first the kingdom of God and His righteousness, and all these things will be provided for you" (Matthew 6:31–33).

Jesus flatly stated, "Don't worry." That's a biblical injunction against worry: just don't do it. It's easier said than done, of course. Many people are chronic worriers; as soon as one worry is resolved, they look for the next thing to worry about. It seems to be a disease that is growing in our society. After all, the American way is self-sufficiency, looking out for No. 1, rugged pioneer independence, and all that. There's no doubt that the world's approach is do it yourself and depend on no one.

Which brings us back to the question, will you trust God to provide for your needs or will you devote your resources to providing them for yourself? Trusting yourself leads to anxiety and worry when you feel that you aren't getting all you need (or want). It also prevents you from seeking God's kingdom first because you're too busy providing for your needs to make God your top priority.

Trusting God, on the other hand, frees you from the desires and trappings of the world. When you gladly accept whatever comes from

God's hand, you realize that He's got it handled better than you ever could. By seeking His kingdom and righteousness first, you can rest assured that "all these things will be provided for you."

Worry and anxiety are based on fear—fear that you won't have what you need. God's love can overcome that when you completely love Him in return. As the apostle John wrote, "There is no fear in love; instead, perfect love drives out fear, because fear involves punishment" (1 John 4:18).

Food or Words?

As always, God wants us to step up a level. He knows that we are always better off when we focus on Him instead of ourselves. In this case, He wants us to consider the most important things He gives us, things that are even more important than food.

Job said, "I have not departed from the commands of His lips; I have treasured the words of His mouth more than my daily food" (Job 23:12). In resisting Satan's first temptation, Jesus quoted Deuteronomy 8:3: "Then Jesus was led up by the Spirit into the wilderness to be tempted by the Devil. After He had fasted 40 days and 40 nights, He was hungry. Then the tempter approached Him and said, 'If You are the Son of God, tell these stones to become bread.' But He answered, 'It is written: Man must not live on bread alone but on every word that comes from the mouth of God'" (Matthew 4:1–4).

Another time Jesus said, "My food is to do the will of Him who sent Me and to finish His work" (John 4:34).

The clear point is that we need God's word and will more than we need food. God will provide for our needs, but He wants us to regard our relationship with Him as more important than anything else, including the food we eat, the clothes we wear, even the air we breathe. When you depend on God fully, He will supply all these things.

It should be obvious that taking this approach goes hand in glove with being intimate with God. It's one more aspect of a close, loving relationship with your heavenly Father. The closer you are to Him, the more evident His provision for your life. And the more you will perceive His word as more important than all of your earthly needs put together.

The Rest of the Story

I began this chapter with our tithing experience. It was so exciting that I decided to figure out how God had done it. I took our financial records—receipts, income statements, credit card statements, offering records, cancelled checks, I had them all—and began calculating. *Shouldn't take long*, I thought. But after a week of poring over three years of records, I couldn't solve the puzzle. It was easy enough to explain how we had gotten into debt, but I had no clue how God had gotten us out.

I need to make a point: I like math. It was always my favorite subject in school and my major when I graduated from college. For six years I taught high school math. I still enjoy solving math problems and puzzles. I'm telling you that simply to say that I had every reason to believe that I could solve this mystery. *Should be obvious*, I thought.

So I tried again. And again. On three separate occasions, in various ways, I tried to determine what God had done. My conclusion, no matter what approach I used, was that there was no earthly reason that we should have eliminated our debt. In fact, the numbers showed it should have kept growing. From a human perspective, it just didn't make any sense.

I finally realized that God was not going to allow me to understand what had happened by examining the data, no matter how smart I thought I was. Instead, He was telling me to simply trust Him to provide for my family's needs, and that by faithfully serving and obeying Him, He would lead us through the problems of life. We haven't always done that perfectly, but the more we have trusted Him (and not ourselves), the more clearly He has proven Himself to be trustworthy.

Am I saying that if you're drowning in debt, all you need to do is begin tithing and soon your money worries will be over? Not necessarily.

I don't know that God will do the same in your case as He did in ours. Maybe He has a different lesson for you to learn. Maybe He can work His will even though you're in debt. Maybe He'll do even more for you than He did for us. It's not for me to say exactly how God wants to work in your life. All I can say for sure is what the Bible tells us: when you fully trust God and depend on Him, He supplies all your needs.

Praying for God's Provision

Here are some specific ways to ask God to provide for you:

» Make a list of your daily physical needs, ask God to provide them, and tell Him that you want to fully trust Him. Do the same exercise for your daily mental, emotional, financial, and social needs.

» Ask God for the ability to fully trust Him for all your needs.

» Ask God to remove worry and anxiety from your mind by helping you see how fully He can provide in any situation.

» Ask God to show you any ways in which you trust yourself for the things for which you should be trusting Him. Pray that you can take the focus off yourself and let God provide.

» You need much more than just food to survive and thrive.

» God supplies all your needs according to His purposes and in His time.

» Worry and anxiety are eliminated when you completely trust God.

» God wants you to focus on His word and will instead of yourself and your needs.

» You must depend on God, even when you don't get all the answers.

» Main point: When you trust in God and depend completely on Him, He continually supplies all your needs.

PURSUING PERFECT* PASSION

For personal or group study

1. What has been your overall experience with trusting God to provide your life's needs? How dependent have you been on God? How faithful has He been to provide for you?

2. Read John 6:1–14,22–40. What does this story have to do with depending on God for our daily needs? What can we learn from it?

3. Read Proverbs 10:24. How does one's righteousness play a part in receiving provision from God? Is God's provision dependent on our doing His will?

4. How difficult is it for you to distinguish between your needs and wants? To what extent does God provide what you need? To what extent does He provide what you want?

5. How can trusting in God on a daily basis help us learn to trust Him more? Is it really that important to make this a daily exercise?

6. Have you ever had an extremely pressing need? As your unmet need became more urgent, even critical, was it easier or harder to trust God to provide? How does your level of dependence on God play into your level of faith in Him?

7. As one's trust in God for His provision grows, does one's level of need increase or decrease? In other words, can we get by with less if we trust God more? Can you find any biblical support for this idea?

8. Do you agree that worry is equivalent to a lack of trust in God? Why or why not?

9. Do you agree that love for God will overcome fear and worry?
    Why or why not?

10. To what extent is worry a problem for you? Do you feel a need
    to address your level of anxiety? What steps do you believe God
    would have you take?

11. Has it been your experience that seeking God's kingdom first
    enables Him to provide for you even more? What do you believe
    is the relationship between these two things in God's mind?

12. How comfortable are you with the idea that we need God's
    word more than we need food? Does that concept change your
    perspective on life?

9

Your Sin: God's Pardon

And forgive us our debts, as we also have forgiven our debtors.
—Matthew 6:12

CALL SOMEONE A SINNER IN today's world, and you may get a harsh response. You may be accused of being intolerant or hypocritical. No one wants to be deemed sinful, it seems. As someone once told me, "I'm not a sinner! I'm just as good as everyone else!" While she undoubtedly is as good as everyone else, the problem is that everyone else is not so good. The fact is that everyone is a sinner. As Paul put it, "All have sinned and fall short of the glory of God" (Romans 3:23).

In Chapter 1 we saw that there is one exception to that rule. But Jesus wasn't sinless because He was never tempted to sin. Early in His ministry, Jesus was tempted by Satan: "Then Jesus was led up by the Spirit into the wilderness to be tempted by the Devil" (Matthew 4:1). Undoubtedly Jesus was regularly tempted to turn His ministry into something less than God had planned, but He always resisted those temptations. The writer of Hebrews said that Jesus "has been tested in every way as we are, yet without sin" (Hebrews 4:15).

As Satan tempted Jesus, we are all tempted to sin against God. But temptation isn't sin. Just because an evil thought comes to mind doesn't mean you have to act on it. You don't have to lust simply because you see someone attractive. You don't have to lie your way out of a sticky situation just because you can.

Yes, temptation is the path to sin, but you don't have to walk that path. We must frequently decide which path to take, and we need to know that temptation is always near, luring us in the wrong direction.

Sin? What's That?

What is sin, then? In the Bible, various words and phrases are used to connote the idea of sin. Here are some of their meanings (including example verses):

» Missing the mark or coming up short, based on the idea of an arrow missing the target (see Exodus 32:30)

» Breaking the law, specifically the laws God gave through Moses; transgression against God (see Matthew 15:3)

» Acting wickedly (see Nehemiah 9:33)

» Rebelling against God or others; trespassing (see Isaiah 1:2)

» Veering away from the proper path (see Deuteronomy 5:32)

» Behaving in a morally corrupt or evil fashion (see 2 Samuel 7:14)

» Incurring a moral debt (see Philemon 1:18)

Jesus used the idea of incurring a debt in the Model Prayer. He said that we need to ask forgiveness for that debt. When you behave in a way that doesn't match what God has in mind, you have incurred a moral debt, and you owe it to God. Since you aren't God, you have no intrinsic righteousness from which to pay, so you need God to forgive the debt.

No matter what word picture or concept you use, it's clear that we are sinning any time we don't fulfill all that God has planned for us. The essence of sin is to love self more than God and thus choose self over God. Stated that way, it's easy to see why everyone sins because we regularly choose to satisfy our own selfish desires. It's sad but true that our earthly nature leads us to love ourselves more than we love intimacy with God.

Consider the original sin as an example of love for self. When Satan tempted Eve, he directed her focus to what the fruit could do for her and not on what God had said about it.

> The woman said to the serpent, "We may eat the fruit from the trees in the garden. But about the fruit of the tree in the middle of the garden, God said, 'You must not eat it or touch it, or you will die.'"

> "No! You will not die," the serpent said to the woman. "In fact, God knows that when you eat it your eyes will be opened and you will be like God, knowing good and evil." Then the woman saw that the tree was good for food and delightful to look at, and that it was desirable for obtaining wisdom. So she took some of its fruit and at it; she also gave some to her husband, who was with her, and he ate it. (Genesis 3:2–6)

Adam and Eve's actions were based on what benefit they thought they could derive from eating the fruit, regardless of what God had said. They conveniently forgot the fact that they had all the fruit they needed from every other tree in the garden. Instead, they wanted more for themselves. Their selfish approach caused them to disobey God's command to not eat fruit from that specific tree. They apparently loved satisfying their desires more than they loved intimacy with God.

Look at the sins that Paul instructed the Galatian church to avoid: "Now the works of the flesh are obvious: sexual immortality, moral impurity, promiscuity, idolatry, sorcery, hatreds, strife, jealousy, outbursts of anger, selfish ambitions, dissensions, factions, envy, drunkenness, carousing, and anything similar…" (Galatians 5:19–21).

Every one of these sins is sourced in selfishness and self-focus. We choose to commit them because we love ourselves and want to serve ourselves instead of serving God. That's the essence of sin. The result is that we dishonor God by our own selfish actions, and we put distance between ourselves and Him.

God knows what we are like, of course. That's why He provided a way to receive forgiveness for our sins. The way of forgiveness, which we discussed in previous chapters, is based on His love, mercy, and grace. Fortunately for us, God loves us enough to provide that forgiveness, because we all need it.

Why You Need to Ask Forgiveness

As mentioned previously, there are two kinds of people in the world: those who have a relationship with God and those who don't. The Bible calls the first group "saved" and the others "lost." The fundamental difference is that saved people (a.k.a. Christians) have recognized that their sin separates them from God and have trusted Jesus' sacrifice on the cross to provide forgiveness for those sins. God has established a father-child relationship, making every saved person His child. Lost people do not have that relationship because they have not accepted God's forgiveness.

If you are a Christian, it is important to understand that God has forgiven all your sins—not only your past sins but your future ones as well. You don't have to worry about losing your relationship with God because His forgiveness covers *all* your sins. However, your sins can certainly cause your intimacy with God to suffer.

Here's an illustration. I have two sons. Both live in different cities from me, and our relationships are good, so this is a hypothetical example. If one son daily communicates with me, working with me on projects and enjoying our time together, then the relationship will be vibrant, rewarding, and fulfilling for both of us. If the other one never calls, visits, or spends time with me, then the relationship will be cold, lifeless, and unfulfilling. But they will both still be my sons.

No matter how much the first one tries, he can't become my son any more than he already is. And just because the relationship is strained and needs refreshing, it doesn't mean that the other one stops being my son. To be sure, forgiveness and grace may be needed to restore the vitality of the relationship, but he's still my son forever. Nothing can change that.

In the same way, no matter how much I ignore and dishonor God, I'm still going to be His child—a disobedient child in need of severe discipline, perhaps, but still His child.

A similar analogy is the husband-wife relationship. I love my wife, Mary, more than life itself, but sometimes I say or do something that hurts her. When I hurt her, in essence I've sinned against her, so I need her forgiveness. However, I am still her husband. I have hurt Mary, damaged our relationship, and negatively impacted our intimacy, but we are still married. Once I come to my senses and ask her to forgive me, she does and our relationship can then begin to heal and flourish again.

In the same way, when you sin as a Christian, you damage your relationship with God and negatively impact its intimacy. In a sense, you move away from God when you sin; you aren't as close as you were before. Your unforgiven sin will affect your prayer life, worship, and relationship with other Christians. Your testimony for God won't be nearly as effective, especially if others know your sin and label you as a hypocrite. Your life as a Christian is always weakened when you sin.

That's why you need to ask forgiveness for your sins. It isn't because you've lost your salvation or are no longer God's child. It is precisely *because* you are God's child that you need forgiveness so that your intimacy with God can be restored. You can draw close to Him again. When the debt has been cleared, nothing can hinder your love relationship with your heavenly Father.

The great thing about asking for forgiveness is that God always forgives you when you ask! "If we confess our sins, He is faithful and righteous to forgive us our sins and to cleanse us from all unrighteousness" (1 John 1:9).

Implicit in your request for forgiveness is the acknowledgement that you have sinned. The word "confess" means "say together." To confess a sin means to say the same thing God says: you have done something wrong. Asking for forgiveness is a tacit admission that you have sinned, and He is "faithful and righteous to forgive"—and not only to forgive your sin but to cleanse you from unrighteousness. God restores the freshness of your relationship by making you perfect* again!

God Expects You to Forgive Others

We need to note that once Jesus finished the Model Prayer, He immediately commented on the idea of forgiving other people: "And forgive us our debts, as we also have forgiven our debtors ... For if you forgive people their wrongdoing, your heavenly Father will forgive you as well. But if you don't forgive people, your Father will not forgive your wrongdoing" (Matthew 6:12,14–15).

Jesus clearly says that we must forgive others to receive God's forgiveness. How can that be? Are we really forgiven only if we forgive others?

Let's remind ourselves that there are two kinds of forgiveness: the kind we need to be forgiven for all our sins and saved, and the kind we need to restore our intimacy with God. Nowhere in the Bible does God indicate that we must forgive others to be saved. The only requirement to receive God's saving grace is to put your faith in Jesus as your Savior. "For by grace you are saved through faith, and this is not from yourselves; it is God's gift—not from works, so that no one can boast" (Ephesians 2:8–9). "For God loved the world in this way: He gave His One and Only Son, so that everyone who believes in Him will not perish but have eternal life" (John 3:16).

Once you accept God's love and grace, remember, you become part of God's family. He's your Father, you're His child, and you now have many brothers and sisters. It is the people who sin against you whom you are to forgive. But if you don't have a spirit of forgiveness for others, how will you be able to experience God's mercy for you?

Jesus made the very same point in a parable one day.

Then Peter came to Him and said, "Lord, how many times could my brother sin against me and I forgive him? As many as seven times?"

"I tell you, not as many as seven," Jesus said to him, "but 70 times seven. For this reason, the kingdom of heaven can be compared to a king who wanted to settle accounts with his slaves. When he began to settle accounts, one who owed 10,000 talents was brought before him. Since he had no way to pay it back, his master commanded that he, his wife, his children, and everything he had be sold to pay the debt.

"At this, the slave fell facedown before him and said, 'Be patient with me, and I will pay you everything!' Then the master of that slave had compassion, released him, and forgave him the loan.

"But that slave went out and found one of his fellow slaves who owed him 100 denarii. He grabbed him, started choking him, and said, 'Pay what you owe!'

"At this, his fellow slave fell down and began begging him, 'Be patient with me, and I will pay you back.' But he wasn't willing. On the contrary, he went and threw him into prison until he could pay what was owed. When the other slaves saw what had taken place, they were deeply distressed and went and reported to their master everything that had happened.

"Then, after he had summoned him, his master said to him, 'You wicked slave! I forgave you all that debt because you begged me. Shouldn't you also have had mercy on your fellow slave, as I had mercy on you?' And his master got angry and handed him over to the jailers until he could pay everything that was owed. So My heavenly Father will also do to you if each of you does not forgive his brother from his heart." (Matthew 18:21–35)

Peter must have thought he was demonstrating an enormous amount of mercy when he suggested that he would forgive someone seven times. (Come to think of it, how many of us would be willing to forgive someone seven times?)

Jesus wasn't impressed, though. He essentially told Peter to forgive until he lost count (i.e., forgive as much as is needed). Then He told a striking parable to drive home the point.

A denarius was about a day's wage for a common worker. So the second slave owed the equivalent of about four months' wages—let's say $20,000 today. Not a trivial amount for most of us. But how much had the first slaved owed his master? A talent was the equivalent of about six thousand denarii, so he owed more like $12 billion—an amount that he had no hope of ever repaying even though he begged for the chance. Because his master was compassionate, he had been forgiven a huge amount, but he wasn't willing to forgive his fellow slave even a tiny fraction of that. He had received great grace, but he wasn't willing to extend that grace at all.

The message is clear: we are to offer grace to those around us because God has dealt graciously with us. Whatever wrongdoings we experience are negligible compared with how much forgiveness we have received from God.

I recently saw a television commercial in which a woman stopped a man from absentmindedly walking in front of a bus. A bystander noticed, and the next scene showed him doing a good deed for another. This chain of good deeds continued several more times. At the end of the commercial, viewers were encouraged to help other people when the opportunity arises. The point was that good deeds can be contagious and that we all benefit when we help another person in need.

The same is true with forgiveness. You are never more like God than when you practice His brand of love, mercy, and forgiveness. So not only does forgiving others open you to receive God's forgiveness, it also encourages those you forgive to keep the ball rolling and forgive others around them. What a great commercial that would be!

Forgive and Forget

You've probably heard someone say, "I'll forgive, but I'll never forget." The person has been hurt so badly that he can't forget the pain. The problem is that he is only pretending to forgive.

That's not God's way. Real forgiveness forgets. He doesn't hold grudges, and neither should we. If you forgive someone, it's also time to forget. Remember, God has forgiven you so thoroughly that He has forgotten your sins. "For I will forgive their wrongdoing and never again remember their sin" (Jeremiah 31:34). "As far as the east is from the west, so far has He removed our transgressions from us" (Psalm 103:12).

I don't know about you, but for me that's a huge amount of mercy and grace. There's no way that the total sum of grace I extend to others could ever come close to matching what God has provided for me. I owe it to Him to forgive my debtors, no matter how many times.

If you are holding a grudge against someone, you need to understand that you are harming yourself. Just like anxiety and worry, pent-up anger and resentment can cause disease and pain. Holding a grudge is a sure way to hurt yourself even more than you hurt the other person. By offering forgiveness, you will undoubtedly prevent untold harm to yourself and those around you. In addition, you might possibly help restore a valuable relationship, you will demonstrate obedience to God's commands, and you will become more like Jesus.

You see, God doesn't want any Hatfield-McCoy feuds in His kingdom. He wants His children to love each other just as much as He loves us. Only in this way can we fulfill God's desire for us to become like Jesus. If we truly love our brothers and sisters in Christ, we will be willing to forgive them "seventy times seven." And forget every one of those, too.

Praying for God's Pardon

Try these suggestions as you pray for pardon for your sins:

» Ask God to show you your sins. Seek to listen long enough to hear the details. Ask especially for God to reveal any blind spots that you may have regarding sin.

» Ask God to forgive your sins, and then listen for His assurance that He has forgiven you.

» Thank God that He has forgiven your sins and that you do not have to repeatedly remember and repent for the same sin.

» Meditate on your relationships and determine whom you have not forgiven. Ask God to lead you to truly forgive those persons.

» Thank God for His forgiveness of your sins. Continue in an attitude of true thankfulness.

CHAPTER SUMMARY

» The essence of sin is to love self more than God.

» You need God's forgiveness for your sins once and for all to become His child.

» You also need God's forgiveness on a continual basis to maintain a close relationship with Him.

» You can't receive God's forgiveness if you aren't willing to forgive others.

» Main point: You continually need God's forgiveness to restore the intimacy of your relationship with Him.

Pursuing Perfect* Passion

For personal or group study

1. Read these Bible passages and list the sins they describe:
   » Exodus 20:1–17 (the Ten Commandments)
   » Matthew 5:21–48) (the Sermon on the Mount)
   » Ephesians 4:25–32
   » Colossians 3:5–9

2. In addition to those listed in question 1, what other Bible passages can you find that list and describe sins?

3. To you, what is the essence of sin? Is it selfishness or is it something else? What's the basis for your answer?

4. What motivates you to sin? What temptations do you find hard to resist? Are there any sins that your regularly commit even though you try hard not to?

5. Some people confess their sins to a priest. Others confess their sins to an accountability partner. How much value would it bring you to confess your sins to another person? Would that person's encouragement help you understand and accept God's forgiveness? If you don't have an accountability partner, consider asking God who might fill that role in your life.

6. How confident are you that God has forgiven all your sins? Are there sins for which you still feel guilty? If so, do you believe that God has forgiven you for those sins? What is the source of your guilt feelings?

7. Are you holding any grudges? Is there anyone you haven't been

able to forgive or don't want to forgive? If so, how does that affect your intimacy with God?

8. Read Luke 23:32–34 and Acts 7:54–60. Do you think that Jesus' words from the cross had anything to do with Stephen's dying words? How do these two examples influence your response to those who have hurt you?

9. Sometimes the family of a murder victim forgives the murderer, and sometimes they desire vengeance. If someone were to murder one of your relatives, what would be your response? Would you be able to forgive them? Why or why not?

10. Has God truly forgotten your sins? Have you forgotten others' sins?

10

YOUR PATH: GOD'S PRESENCE

And do not bring us into temptation.
—Matthew 6:13

A s my two brothers and I were growing up, Mom regularly took us to the local toy store to check out all the neat stuff. Footballs, baseballs and bats, toy soldiers and tanks, model cars, board games, baseball cards, all the different kinds of bubble gum and candy— whatever a six-year-old boy could want, they had it. With our allowances my brothers and I could usually afford an item or two each week, or we could save up for weeks for something bigger (a concept that regularly escaped me for some reason).

One day, as I surveyed the toy cars and trucks, I happened to notice a little game. Not just little, tiny. It was a Scrabble game, a perfect reproduction from the game board right down to the tiny letter tiles and wooden racks. I was captivated by this amazing miniature. It was part of a much bigger set of replicas in some kind of toy playhouse, none of the details of which I remember. But I do remember everything about that Scrabble game. It came in a little box only two inches across, but I could read each letter and its point value perfectly. Even the squares on the game board were the appropriate colors.

Week after week I studied that Scrabble game. I knew I would never have enough money to buy the playhouse, and I had no interest in the rest of it anyway. But did I want that game. I thought about it every day. I'm sure that Mom got tired of hearing me describe it. For whatever reason, I was obsessed with that miniature game, and I constantly dreamed of playing with it. I began to wonder if it would be missed if someone surreptitiously acquired it. That game was screaming my name!

So I took matters into my own hands. One day, when I was sure that no one was watching, I took the game and stuck it in my pocket. I immediately felt pangs of guilt, and I was certain that the store clerk scrutinized me as I walked out, but the deed was done. I took the game home and hid it in my room. After a couple days, when the coast was clear, I pulled it out and played Scrabble with an imaginary opponent. I still felt guilty, but I was enjoying the game.

It wasn't long before the inevitable happened and Mom caught me. I don't know if she was clever enough or if my brother ratted me out. Either way, the punishment was swift and painful. But the worst part was that I had to return the game to the store owner and apologize. I remember the extreme embarrassment just as clearly as the game itself—my first experience with shoplifting, and I was caught red-handed by my own mother. (First *and* last, let me hasten to add.) I'm not sure that I learned any big lesson at the time, but it wasn't hard to figure out that giving in to temptation will eventually bring pain.

As noted in the previous chapter, temptation isn't sin, but it leads directly to sin. We experience temptation daily, and most of us have some temptations that are difficult to resist. It seems that we need a lot of help overcoming temptation.

It would also seem that God has a vested interest in His children doing the right thing and not sinning, so we wonder why we have to ask God not to bring us into temptation. Is He normally inclined to cause us to be tempted so we need to ask Him not to do that? Does God derive some secret pleasure from watching us sin so that He can cast judgment on us? Is He somehow in league with Satan to do His best to trip us up and condemn us after all?

The answer to these questions is, "Don't be ridiculous—of course not!" God doesn't make us His children to torture us. He loves us and wants us to overcome temptation and obey Him.

Trials and Temptations

James, the brother of Jesus, gives us good advice in this matter:

> Consider it a great joy, my brothers, whenever you experience various trials, knowing that the testing of your faith produces endurance. But endurance must do its complete work, so that you may be mature and complete, lacking nothing … Blessed is a man who endures trials, because when he passes the test he will receive the crown of life that He has promised to those who love Him. No one undergoing a trial should say, "I am being tempted by God." For God is not tempted by evil, and He Himself doesn't tempt anyone. But each person is tempted when he is drawn away and enticed by his own evil desires. Then after desire has conceived, it gives birth to sin, and when sin is fully grown, it gives birth to death. (James 1:2–4,12–15)

There are several important points in this passage. First, note that the root word for trials is the same as for temptations. Trials and temptations are identical from our standpoint. Both are occasions to resist doing the easy thing and instead stay on a path that is true to God, and we must choose between the two. If we make the wrong choice, we sin. If we choose well, we become more like Jesus, who never once gave in to temptation.

James claims that we should think of trials as a good thing—"a great joy"—because the testing leads to endurance and maturity. We normally don't consider life's difficulties to be a source of joy, but by taking the long-term view, we see that James is right. Only by persevering through the trials of life can we mature. The word translated "mature" in verse 4 is *teleios*, which you may remember can also be translated as "perfect." Our journey through life should result in a greater maturity as we grow to be more like Jesus, our example of perfection.

James' main point is that life's trials help us to grow as we learn by experience the difference between right and wrong. But we must face these trials with faith in God so that we have His help. Just as a child moves to a higher grade by passing the test, you mature toward perfection* by passing life's tests.

As pastor of the Jerusalem church, James had plenty of experience on which to draw. Within a few years of the church's beginning, widespread persecution became the norm, and the Jerusalem Christians regularly faced many types of difficulty. Jerusalem was still the seat of Judaism, and the Jewish leaders never gave up trying to stamp out what they thought was a dangerous cult. Church members were criticized, ostracized, harassed, fired from their jobs, and even attacked and beaten. Only by facing these challenges with God's power could James and the other Christians even hope to survive.

When you stop to think about it, it's clear that we never learn much from the good times. When life feels like a casual stroll through a grassy park with the sun shining and flowers blooming, the birds singing and children laughing, why would anyone consider changing? But no change means no growth. It is when the sunny skies turn to dark storms that we realize that change is necessary, and by making the right changes we grow stronger and more mature. We learn how to respond when things aren't going well. Perhaps most importantly, we learn that life is *not* a walk in the park and that we must be prepared to deal with difficulties if we don't want to end up overwhelmed by the storms.

As James says, God doesn't tempt us to sin. That makes sense because sin is disobedience to God, and He wouldn't lead someone that way. Instead, God allows you to be tested to prove your faith, increase your endurance, and lead you to maturity.

What then is the source of these trials and temptations? We know that God doesn't tempt us, but Satan does. And as James said, we are tempted by our own evil desires. Selfish motives are the source of our sin, as we saw in detail in Chapter 9. We see things we want and seek after them rather than depending on God to provide for our needs. By doing so we begin to walk our own path—the path of sin.

Experiencing Trials

Looking back at our focal verse, the same root word is used for temptation. Matthew 6:13 could therefore read "and do not bring us into a trial." The concept is that of being put to the test. The motivation for the test could be evil, as when Satan tries to trip you up by tempting you to sin. It could also be good, as when you get the chance to overcome the temptation and avoid sin.

Although God doesn't tempt you to sin, He does allow you to be tested by facing temptation. His goal is not to cause you to stumble but to give you an opportunity to put your faith in His ability to see you through the trial. "No temptation has overtaken you except what is common to humanity. God is faithful and He will not allow you to be tempted beyond what you are able, but with the temptation He will also provide a way of escape, so that you are able to bear it" (1 Corinthians 10:13).

Thus we see that, from a human perspective, a trial is the same as a temptation: an opportunity to make a choice either for or against God. When tempted, we choose to obey and follow God and keep walking with Him or we choose to disobey and go our own way, which means that we are following self, Satan, and the world.

By asking God not to bring us into temptation, we admit our penchant for making the wrong choice, but we also show our desire to walk with Him. Therefore, we want to minimize the opportunities to take the wrong path. We know that temptations will occur anyway and that we will need to discipline ourselves to endure, but we are more likely to stay on God's path if we don't have to make the choice. When there is no test, there is no chance of failure.

By praying "Do not bring me into temptation," I am essentially saying to God, "Look, Lord, I really want to walk with You on the path that You are on, so if there are no other options that appear, I'm a lot more likely to stay with You. If trials show up, so that I can choose to leave You, it's very possible that I will go down the wrong path. So please don't bring me to a place where an alternate path presents itself. Let me just walk with You without any chance of failure."

This may seem like a naïve approach, but it does take our human nature into account. As is so frequently pointed out in the Bible, we are a lot like sheep—too dumb to know the right way to go and ready to veer off at any point. We regularly go off the path and get lost, wandering into trials, trouble, testing, and temptation. We need the Shepherd to guide us. We're also sometimes like fish—ready to chase any bright, shiny object that appears whether or not there is a hook behind it. We need to follow God's path, so we should ask for minimal risk.

From a more positive standpoint, we're asking God to take us wherever He wants us to go—all the great possibilities at His disposal to do His perfect will. It's like saying, "Take me anywhere and everywhere, Lord, just not to a place of possible failure."

We've already prayed for His glory, kingdom, and will. We've asked for His provision and pardon. It would be great to not have to ask for Him to forgive us for yet another failure. Instead, we want to follow Him obediently and joyfully into whatever adventure He has to provide for us. As David said, "The Lord is my shepherd; there is nothing I lack. He lets me lie down in green pastures; He leads me beside quiet waters. He renews my life; He leads me along the right paths for His name's sake" (Psalm 23:1–3).

God is ready and willing to lead us. He is our Shepherd. We need those green pastures, quiet waters, and right paths in our lives, so it is appropriate to ask God to keep us away from roaring rapids, steep cliffs, and ravenous wolves—and miniature Scrabble games.

An Important Conjunction

Our focal verse begins with a conjunction: *"And* do not bring us into temptation." Jesus wasn't one to waste any words. The "and" is not there just to take up space; it indicates an important union of thoughts.

Think of it this way. You just admitted to God in verse 12 that you have sinned and need His forgiveness. You realize that taking the wrong path always leads to bad results, so you should ask God to minimize the possibility of leaving His side to pursue your own selfish ways. In essence you are saying, "Father, thank You for forgiving my sins. Now help me keep from sinning against You. Don't give me any opportunities to fail. There will be enough chances to sin because of my own selfish nature, Satan's efforts to derail me, and the world's enticements. I know that they will come anyway, but please reduce the number to a minimum. Lead me in ways that help me to succeed in my walk with You."

By seeing the relationship between these two thoughts, you can better understand the need for asking God not to bring you into temptation.

Why Testing Can Lead to Celebrating

Moses is a great example of someone who was devoted to God yet experienced all kinds of difficulty because of that devotion. He was faithful, but Pharaoh was recalcitrant, the Israelites rebellious, and the Canaanites ferocious. Even his own brother and sister complained about his leadership.

Nevertheless, Moses continued to walk with God, and that path held the real rewards. Because God called Moses into His presence, his very appearance was changed. "But whenever Moses went before the Lord to speak with Him, he would remove the veil until he came out. After he came out, he would tell the Israelites what he had been commanded, and the Israelites would see that Moses' face was radiant. Then Moses would put the veil over his face again until he went to speak with the Lord" (Exodus 34:34–35).

Being in God's presence is its own reward. Your face may not begin to glow, but God's radiance will shine through in other ways if you are intimate with Him. As we've seen before, our relationship with God causes us to take on His attributes, and that's cause for celebration.

But how can trials and temptation make us want to celebrate? We already know that our natural inclination is to take our own path, which is invariably the wrong one. Thus, temptation is simply a natural outgrowth of the way we normally approach life. We've seen that testing can help us mature by learning a different response, so as James said, we can consider it a great joy—if we make the right choice and remain in God's presence.

Another reason to celebrate temptation is that Satan doesn't waste much time tempting people who are already on the wrong path. He spends his greatest energy tempting obedient Christians. Why? So that he can cause us to stumble and thus influence others to see us as hypocrites and keep them from wanting to join us.

Satan tried his best to tempt Jesus to sin but failed miserably. Since he got nowhere with Jesus, his next best idea is to get His strongest followers to sin. If you are undergoing great temptation, it may be because Satan is trying with all his might to pull you away from God. It's one confirmation that you are on the right path if Satan is trying to entice you away from it.

Finally, remember that God allows testing in our lives because He is motivated by love. A good parent is proud when his child shows maturity in a trying situation, and God is no different. Since Jesus confirmed that loving God is His primary command, our best choice is always to prove our love by our actions.

We continually have opportunities to mature. Satan is trying his best to tempt us if we are close to God, and God gives us chances to prove our love for Him. Let's celebrate the great joy that God gives us by thanking Him for the chance to succeed and His power to do so.

Staying Awake

Jesus used the word "temptation" when talking with His disciples the night He was betrayed. After telling them to wait, He went farther into the Garden of Gethsemane and prayed. He returned to find them asleep. "Then He came to the disciples and found them sleeping. He asked Peter, 'So, couldn't you stay awake with Me one hour? Stay awake and pray, so that you won't enter into temptation. The spirit is willing, but the flesh is weak'" (Matthew 26:40–41).

Jesus told Peter and the others that they needed to pray so they wouldn't enter into temptation. The implication was that if they let their guard down, they would walk directly into a trial, and that is exactly what happened.

When Judas arrived with the mob, the disciples put up token opposition before turning and running, leaving Jesus to His captors. Perhaps that's not surprising, considering that the disciples were greatly outnumbered. But it's significant because, just a few hours before, they had been so boastful of their courage"

> Then Jesus said to them, "Tonight all of you will run away because of Me, for it is written: 'I will strike the shepherd, and the sheep of the flock will be scattered.' But after I have been resurrected, I will go ahead of you to Galilee."
>
> Peter told Him, "Even if everyone runs away because of You, I will never run away!"
>
> "I assure you," Jesus said to him, "tonight—before the rooster crows, you will deny Me three times!"
>
> "Even if I have to die with You," Peter told Him, "I will never deny You!" And all the disciples said the same thing. (Matthew 26:31–35)

We're just like those disciples, thinking that we have it all sewn up, that nothing can tempt us because we're so spiritually mature. But just like Peter and the others, we can easily be deceived into trusting our own strength, and it never proves to be enough.

The answer to this dilemma, as Jesus said, is to "stay awake and pray." If we are watching instead of sleeping and praying for guidance and power rather than depending on ourselves, then we will be fully prepared when temptation strikes. By staying in God's presence, we walk the path of continual joy and triumph over temptation.

Praying for God's Presence

Here are some ideas you can try when praying for God's presence:

» Ask God to help you discern tests when they come. Regularly check back with Him to seek to understand their sources, their dangers, and which path you should take.

» Thank God for the trials that come into your life and the opportunity they bring to show your love for Him.

» Ask God to show you the path you have taken with Him and listen as He reveals His work. Thank Him for His presence and power. Commit to seek greater intimacy as He leads you into the future.

» When facing temptation, try to experience God's joy by listening for His voice. Seek to grow closer to God by enjoying His presence. Celebrate His strength that works through you to endure the test.

» Ask God to show you what temptations you may be sleeping through and to help you to stay awake and watchful.

CHAPTER SUMMARY

» Through the difficulty they bring, trials teach us to overcome, grow, and mature in our relationship with God.

» Ask God to lead you every step of the path but include a minimum of trials, testing, and temptation.

» Testing can lead to celebrating and great joy when we pass the test.

» We must stay awake and pray in order to conquer temptation.

» Main point: Ask God to not bring you into testing but instead to lead you along His paths of righteousness.

PURSUING PERFECT* PASSION

For personal or group study

1. What are your greatest temptations? How do you normally try to handle them? What's your success rate?

2. Do you ever feel that God is testing you? What kinds of tests do you experience? How well do you usually handle these tests?

3. How strange does it seem to you to rejoice when facing difficulty? In what ways could you personally derive joy from trials and testing?

4. Study the lives of people who depended on God's presence. List the specific ways they turned to God during testing. Here are a few examples to begin with:

    »   Abraham (Genesis 12–23)

    »   Joseph (Genesis 37–46)

    »   David (1 Samuel 16–24)

    »   Job (Job 1–42)

    »   Peter (Acts 1–12)

    »   Paul (Acts 9–28)

5. Do you feel God's presence more clearly at some times than at others? At what points do you feel most intimate with God? When do you feel farther away? What determines how close you feel to God? What can you do to move closer to God more often?

6. In what ways does God's presence strengthen you against trials and temptations?

7. Do you believe that the concept of celebrating through temptation is biblical? What passages can you find to support or to refute it?

8. Try to recall a time when you experienced difficulty, depended on God's presence, and came through stronger and more mature. Were you able to celebrate the experience? How did you celebrate?

9. How hard is it for you to "stay awake and pray"? Do you think that you are currently sleeping through a test? How can you tell whether you are truly awake and aware of what's happening?

10. How would you respond to someone who makes the following statement: "Satan doesn't really exist. What you think are temptations are just human nature behaving normally. These impulses are neither good nor bad but just your own preferences at the time."

11. Read Psalm 25, noting especially verses 4–5, 8–9, and 12. What did the psalmist say was needed to receive God's guidance along His paths? How well are you following the paths that God is walking?

11

Your Weakness: God's Protection

But deliver us from the evil one.
—Matthew 6:13

In the movie *Ghostbusters*, four men depended on their own wits and a lot of luck to defeat the evil Gozer and his ghostly minions. *Independence Day* saw a conglomeration of protagonists repel a massive alien attack against Earth. The heroes in *Transformers*, aided by the Autobots, fought against and overcame the Decepticons who threatened to destroy all humanity. Countless other science fiction movies are based on the idea that mere mortals can prevail over a superhuman enemy despite impossible odds. Who wouldn't want to be that kind of hero? Just think of the media attention!

Needless to say, most of us regular humans don't win that kind of battle. It is fortunate that we don't fight against fictitious ghosts, aliens, or robots, but we do face the real enemy, Satan, every day. We don't possess the power, skill, or intelligence to outwit him. He's too smart, cunning, and powerful for anything we can wield against him. Thus, we must look to God for deliverance.

Deliver Us

When an enemy attacks or oppresses, we need deliverance. For example, the book of Exodus tells how God used Moses to deliver the Israelites from their Egyptian tormentors. Although Moses was a reluctant leader, God motivated him to take His message directly to Pharaoh. When Pharaoh increased the oppression in response, Moses predicted a series of ten plagues on Egypt, culminating with the death of all firstborn Egyptian children and animals and the release of the Israelites.

In the early seventh century BC, Jerusalem was attacked by Assyria, an episode described in 2 Kings 18-19. Sennacherib, the Assyrian king, had already conquered the northern kingdom of Israel along with several other nations, and now he turned his attention to Judah. King Hezekiah responded to this threat by going to the temple and pleading with God to intervene. God answered his prayer by destroying the enemy's army and delivering His people.

Acts 12 describes how God miraculously delivered Peter from Herod, who had already martyred the apostle James. After arresting Peter, Herod had him chained and guarded by sixteen soldiers. During the night before the planned execution, God sent an angel to free Peter without the guards even noticing, and the fallout was tremendous.

In these and many other situations described in the Bible, God used His great power to deliver His people from the enemy. To deliver means to release, rescue, set free, or liberate. The word carries the sense of being brought out of danger or captivity.

According to Jesus, those who are captive to sin need to be delivered from it: "As He was saying these things, many believed in Him. So Jesus said to the Jews who had believed Him, 'If you continue in My word, you really are My disciples. You will know the truth, and the truth will set you free.' 'We are descendants of Abraham,' they answered Him, 'and we have never been enslaved to anyone. How can You say, "You will become free?"' Jesus responded, 'I assure you: Everyone who commits sin is a slave of sin'" (John 8:30–34).

We already know that through faith in Jesus we have been set free from sin and can now live in obedience to God. Paul described it as becoming slaves of obedience to God and righteousness.

> Do you not know that if you offer yourselves to someone
> as obedient slaves, you are slaves of that one you obey—
> either of sin leading to death or of obedience leading
> to righteousness? But thank God that, although you
> used to be slaves of sin, you obeyed from the heart
> that pattern of teaching you were entrusted to, and
> having been liberated from sin, you became enslaved to
> righteousness … But now, since you have been liberated
> from sin and become enslaved to God, you have your
> fruit, which results in sanctification—and the end is
> eternal life! (Romans 6:16–18,22)

Since we have been freed from the tyranny of sin, why do we still need deliverance? Who is the enemy that threatens us? Just before stating the Model Prayer, Jesus had said, "Love your enemies and pray for those who persecute you" (Matthew 5:44). We think our enemies are North Korea, Iran, terrorists, evil dictators, bill collectors, gangs, Republicans, Democrats, independents, gays, straights, strangers, neighbors, and just about anyone else. But the truth is that none of these people are our enemies. They never have been and they never will be. After all, God created each and every person to have an intimate relationship with Him. Jesus died for those people as well, so we are to love them and pray for them.

Our only real enemy is Satan, the evil one. He is the one who, as the deceiver, does all he can to influence people away from the way, the truth, and the life. His goal is to prevent people from entering God's kingdom. Satan deceives, distracts, discourages, and destroys. He is the one from whom we need deliverance. That's why we are to ask God to deliver us from the evil one.

The reason we need deliverance is that we are weak and defenseless against Satan's schemes. We've already seen that we are predisposed toward sin. Our own selfish bent causes us to rebel against God on a regular basis. And Satan always seems to be around to aid and abet our efforts to do what our carnal nature desires. We should recognize that he holds no real power over us because, as Paul said above, we are not his slaves but God's. But Satan does have the ability to tempt us to sin and thus harm our relationship with our Father. If we fall prey to his tricks, we help achieve his goals instead of fulfilling God's purposes.

Only God Can Deliver Us

Thus, we need to be aware of Satan's ruse. Peter commanded, "Be sober! Be on the alert! Your adversary the Devil is prowling around like a roaring lion, looking for anyone he can devour" (1 Peter 5:8). Paul instructed us to be clothed in God's armor: "Finally, be strengthened by the Lord and by His vast strength. Put on the full armor of God so that you can stand against the tactics of the Devil" (Ephesians 6:10–11). He went on to describe the various pieces of God's armor that we need. Undoubtedly, we must be prepared to withstand Satan's attacks.

Some believers want to take the idea of spiritual warfare a step further by going on the offensive against Satan. They want to root out evil where it lives. By trying to attack Satan, however, we fall into one more of his traps. It suits his purposes just fine to have us spend our energy trying to bind, rebuke, or cast out him or his demons.

While we are out engaging the enemy, however, we aren't able to do what God really wants, which as we've already seen is to glorify His name, seek His kingdom, and do His will in our lives. By focusing on Satan instead of God, we unwittingly help Satan advance his cause.

Let's be clear here. The Bible plainly describes how Jesus and His followers actively engaged in spiritual warfare on a regular basis. Jesus cast out many demons and gave His disciples the authority to do the same. That activity continued in the early church; the book of Acts documents several cases in which the apostles and others healed people from unclean spirits. You can't read far in the gospels or Acts before you find Jesus and His followers dealing with evil spirits.

But nowhere in the Bible do we see an instance where Jesus or His followers went looking for demons to assault. In every case where Jesus cast out a demon, either the person came to Him, the person was brought to Him, or someone asked Him to come. Jesus didn't go looking for a fight. Being God, He could at any time have dealt with Satan once and for all, but that wasn't His plan. Jesus didn't make spiritual warfare a major focus of His ministry. Instead, in His last words before leaving earth, He emphasized the Great Commission task of preaching the gospel message wherever we go (see Matthew 28:18–20).

In a similar vein, almost all the spiritual armor described by Paul in Ephesians 6 is defensive: the belt of truth, the breastplate of righteousness, the shoes of readiness for the gospel, the shield of faith, and the helmet of salvation. None of those pieces of armor could be used to attack. Their sole purpose is protection. The only exception is the sword of the Spirit, God's word. We are to use what God has already said to aid us in warding off Satan's attacks.

The main point for us as believers is that spiritual warfare consists primarily in depending on God's protection. When we think that we can take on Satan by our own power or that we should help God by binding or rebuking Satan, we are acting in spiritual arrogance and revealing our spiritual ignorance. The Bible makes it clear that we are to resist Satan, not rebuke him: "Therefore, submit to God. But resist the Devil, and he will flee from you" (James 4:7).

Jesus Showed the Way

Let's learn from another example in the life of Christ.

Then Jesus was led up by the Spirit into the wilderness to be tempted by the Devil. After He had fasted 40 days and 40 nights, He was hungry. Then the tempter approached Him and said, "If You are the Son of God, tell these stones to become bread."

But He answered, "It is written: Man must not live on bread alone but on every word that comes from the mouth of God."

Then the Devil took Him to the holy city, had Him stand on the pinnacle of the temple, and said to Him, "If You are the Son of God, throw Yourself down. For it is written: He will give His angels orders concerning you, and they will support you with their hands so that you will not strike your foot against a stone."

Jesus told him, "It is also written: Do not test the Lord your God."

Again the Devil took Him to a very high mountain and showed Him all the kingdoms of the world and their splendor. And he said to Him, "I will give You all these things if You will fall down and worship me."

Then Jesus told him, "Go away, Satan! For it is written: Worship the Lord your God, and serve only Him."

Then the Devil left Him, and immediately angels came and began to serve Him. (Matthew 4:1–11)

Jesus willingly allowed Himself to be attacked by Satan. In the previous chapter, we learned that we should ask God not to bring us into those situations, but in this case the Holy Spirit expressly led Jesus to undergo temptation. The reason is that, at the beginning of His ministry, Jesus needed to eliminate any competing ideas of what that ministry should be. We are told that Satan tempted Jesus in three specific ways in an attempt to get Him to be a messiah who was less than what God purposed:

>> A messiah who meets earthly needs and thus attracts a following, giving people an easy way out of difficult circumstances. Jesus did meet earthly needs on a regular basis, but that was because He was demonstrating His love for people. He knew that we need to be kingdom citizens more than we need solutions for our earthly problems.

>> A messiah who does sensational miracles to prove that He is God. Jesus performed miracles for the purpose of exhibiting God's power, not simply to attract followers.

>> A messiah who rules an earthly kingdom but falls short of His true purpose of dying for mankind. In fact, Jesus now has "all authority ... in heaven and on earth" (Matthew 28:18) and will rule everything at the end of time.

We can learn a lot from this episode. Notice that Satan twice tried to sow a seed of doubt. He is a master at causing us to doubt. It's one of his primary weapons against us. He will try to cause us to doubt ourselves, but mostly he wants us to doubt God, His word, and His promises.

Just like he quoted Psalm 91 in his second temptation, Satan will even quote scripture out of context to mislead us. He directly lied in his third temptation: he does not have authority to give the world to anyone because the world and its kingdoms belong to God. Satan lived up to his name—the deceiver—and he will continually lie to us just like he lied to Jesus. Satan used everything in his power to try to keep Jesus from fulfilling His mission.

It's obvious that Jesus used God's word to deflect Satan's attacks. He quoted three times from the Law in the book of Deuteronomy. Once again we see that we benefit greatly when we know God's word and how to apply it in our lives.

Observe that Jesus didn't spend any time or effort trying to bind or rebuke Satan. He simply depended on His Father and His word to resist Satan's temptations. Once Satan fled, God provided angels to attend to

His needs. In the same way, when we rely on God to deliver us from the evil one, we can be sure that He won't let us down.

Satan will do all he can to keep you from the intimate love relationship that God has for you. He will try to prevent you from fulfilling God's purpose, prioritizing God's kingdom, and doing God's will. He will do everything he can to make you ineffective in your Christian life. In fact, the more intimate you are with God, the more Satan tries to get between you, and the more you need God's deliverance. Only by depending on God can you overcome Satan's schemes.

God Has Already Won the Victory

Most of us would prefer that God protect us, not just from temptation, but from any kind of problem that comes our way: illness, injury, mean neighbors, unemployment, relationship issues, road rage—you name it.

It's true that God can always protect you, but that doesn't mean things will always turn out the way you would like. That's because your life isn't about you; it's about glorifying God. His purpose for your life will not match your earthly view. As we've already seen, His will may include your suffering through some kind of difficulty to help you grow as a Christian and bring greater glory to Him.

That's why Jesus said that to be His follower, you must deny yourself, take up your cross, and follow Him (see Luke 9:23). He followed that approach throughout His life, and perhaps the best example is His prayer in the Garden of Gethsemane. He prayed three times that the "cup" of suffering would pass by him, but He was willing to do what God wanted anyway. "He fell facedown and prayed, 'My Father! If it is possible, let this cup pass from Me. Yet not as I will, but as You will'" (Matthew 26:39). Three times Jesus asked the same thing. And then He submitted to God's will, for which we can be eternally thankful.

Paul said that God had given him a "thorn in the flesh" to keep him humble. He asked three times for the thorn to be removed. "Concerning this, I pleaded with the Lord three times to take it away from me. But He said to me, 'My grace is sufficient for you, for power is perfected in weakness'" (2 Corinthians 12:8–9). Three times he asked. And Christ's response was that His grace was sufficient for Paul to deal with it.

The Father's grace was sufficient for Jesus. Christ's grace was sufficient for Paul. And God's grace is sufficient for you, too, even in the midst of turmoil and suffering. It's not easy to think about suffering, and it's even worse to experience, but no matter what, God is bigger still.

God already has victory over Satan because He is immeasurably stronger. You, however, cannot stand against Satan. Only when you trust in God's power can you overcome Satan in your life. If you fully yield your life to Him, accepting whatever He brings or allows to come into your life, His grace and power will always be sufficient.

More Conjunctions

It seems that Jesus was implying the phrase "when it happens" in this verse: "And do not bring us into temptation, but [when it happens] deliver us from the evil one" (Matthew 6:13). He recognized that the evil one constantly opposes us and seeks to make us fall away from God. A paraphrase could be "and keep us from times of testing, but when they inevitably come anyway, helps us pass the test." Like the "and" at the beginning of the verse that we examined in Chapter 10, this "but" is important because it joins two related phrases.

If we go back yet one more verse we see yet another "and" in a whole series of conjunctions (emphases added): "Give us today our daily bread. *And* forgive us our debts, as we also have forgiven our debtors. *And* do not bring us into temptation, *but* deliver us from the evil one" (Matthew 6:11–13). Thus, verses 11–13 can be viewed as one continuous thread of related requests. Putting them all together, we see this pattern:

> » Father, give us what we need and help us to depend on You for all we need, the most important of which is the opportunity to walk the path that You are already treading. That way we get to continually experience the intimate love relationship which You have initiated with us.

> » And in the cases where we didn't walk with You and instead took the path of selfishness and sin, forgive us. We admit that we have sinned against You and need that forgiveness. Bring us back into close relationship with You.

> » And don't give us additional opportunities to take the wrong path. Minimize the risk for walking away from You and going once again in the wrong direction, leading to sin.

> » But since we'll continually be tested and tempted by the evil one, deliver us by providing the power and wisdom to overcome these temptations and continue to walk with You.

By looking at it this way, we see that the entire Model Prayer is essentially two sides of the same coin. The most important things to God—His glory, kingdom, and will—are made manifest in your life through an intimate, personal relationship with Him. And the fruit of that relationship in your life is that God meets your needs, forgives your sins, leads you on the right path, and protects you from evil.

Your greatest need is to be in God's presence. When you are walking the path with God in a relationship that is based on His love, you begin to understand that everything that is important in life springs from that relationship. Thus, you can devote your entire prayer to maintaining that connection.

No longer must these verses be simply a disjointed series of requests that, though important, can come off as a laundry list of personal demands. Instead, it is once again your relationship with God that is the key to seeing the Model Prayer as a tightly integrated synopsis of life's greatest needs and values.

Finally

"For Yours is the kingdom and the power and the glory forever. Amen" (Matthew 6:13).

The final portion of this verse is omitted from some translations. Since it doesn't appear in some early manuscripts, many scholars believe that it was added later and was not part of Jesus' original prayer. That may be, but still the thought is instructive.

Since the sentence begins with "for," the phrase asserts a reason for praying. If God has the kingdom, power, and glory and He has them forever, why not pray to Him? To whom else can we go for our direction, protection, and provision? There's not a lot more to be said. God has it all, and He has it forever. By recognizing that God is the reason for our existence, we have all the motivation and justification we need for calling to Him in prayer continually throughout our lives.

Praying for God's Protection

Learn to depend on God's protection with these prayer ideas:

» Ask God to show you any ways in which you are falling prey to Satan and then ask for His deliverance in these situations.

» Journal about the times when God delivered you from temptation.

» Depend on God's deliverance when you experience temptations, especially when the temptations are hard for you to overcome.

» Seek to comprehend the working of God's grace through prayer.

Chapter Summary

- » God can deliver His people from attacks and oppression.

- » We are weak and defenseless against Satan and his schemes.

- » Rather than taking the offensive against Satan, spiritual warfare consists mainly in resisting evil and relying on God's protection.

- » Jesus showed us how to resist temptation when Satan attacked Him.

- » God will perfectly protect us by His grace when we depend on Him and not ourselves.

- » Main point: We win the battle against Satan and evil when we depend on God's protection.

Pursuing Perfect* Passion

For personal or group study

1. Can you recall a time when God delivered you from the evil one? What was the situation? What did you have to do? How did God deliver you? What did you learn from the experience?

2. How free are you from the slavery to sin? Are there one or more sins that you find difficult to overcome? Does the thought that you are God's slave help you to grow in sanctification (that is, to become increasingly holy to God) and give you power to resist those sins?

3. "When a man's ways please the Lord, He makes even his enemies to be at peace with him" (Proverbs 16:7). Is there a person whom you consider an enemy? What has this person done that causes you to hold a grudge? Do you pray for that person as Jesus commanded? What would have to happen for you to be at peace with this person?

4. 1 John 4:18 says, "There is no fear in love; instead, perfect love drives out fear, because fear involves punishment." Thus, love should be able to overcome other fear-based tools of Satan, such as anxiety, discouragement, and worry. How does knowing that God's love for you is perfect help you confidently resist Satan and evil?

5. Paul wrapped up his discussion of spiritual armor with an emphasis on prayer (Ephesians 6:18–20). Have you experienced an increased sense of God's protection from the evil one when you pray? How much does prayer factor into your spiritual conflict with Satan?

6. How does your ability to resist temptation compare with Jesus' wilderness experience in Matthew 4:1–11? What can you learn from Jesus to help you resist Satan? Be specific.

7. "The Lord is near all who call out to Him, all who call out to Him with integrity" (Psalm 145:18). Near connotes proximity but can also mean intimacy. Do you feel God's nearness when you call out to Him? If not, what do you need to become more confident in God's convenient and intimate protection?

8. Do you agree that Matthew 6:11–13 can be considered one continuous thought with several related aspects? If so, what is one way that you can apply that in your prayer life? If not, in what way does it help you to consider them as unrelated requests?

Conclusion

Walking with God

I have a little wooden sign on my desk that reads "Exercise daily ... walk with God."

Walking with God is what intimacy is all about. By walking daily with God, you become one with Him. Your heart becomes like His heart. You desire to obey His commands, serve in His kingdom, and glorify His name.

Walking with God was a hallmark of biblical characters who were intimate with God. And when God's people were disobedient, He reproved them for not walking with Him.

> » "Enoch walked with God, and he was not there, because God took him" (Genesis 5:24).
>
> » "Noah was a righteous man, blameless among his contemporaries; Noah walked with God" (Genesis 6:9).
>
> » When Abram was ninety-nine years old, the Lord appeared to him and said, "I am God Almighty; walk before me and be blameless. I will confirm my covenant between me

and you and will greatly increase your numbers" (Genesis 17:1–2 NIV).

» The results for Israel if they obeyed God: "I will walk among you and be your God, and you will be My people" (Leviticus 26:12).

» Moses' command to Israel before they crossed into the Promised Land: "And now, Israel, what does the Lord your God ask of you except to fear the Lord your God by walking in all His ways, to love Him, and to worship the Lord your God with all your heart and all your soul?" (Deuteronomy 10:12).

» Joshua's reminder to the eastern tribes of Israel: "Only carefully obey the command and instruction that Moses the Lord's servant gave you: to love the Lord your God, walk in all His ways, keep His commands, remain faithful to Him, and serve Him with all your heart and all your soul" (Joshua 22:5).

» Jeremiah's portent to Judah in the wake of their disobedience: "However, I did give them this command: 'Obey Me, and then I will be your God, and you will be My people. You must walk in every way I command you so that it may go well with you.' Yet they didn't listen or pay attention but walked according to their own advice and according to their own stubborn, evil heart. They went backward and not forward" (Jeremiah 7:23–24).

» Micah's summary of God's word to Israel through His prophets in the eighth century BC: "He has told you men what is good and what it is the Lord requires of you: Only to act justly, to love faithfulness, and to walk humbly with your God" (Micah 6:8).

The goal of this book has been to help you learn what Jesus has to teach you about building intimacy with God through prayer. Jesus clearly walked with God throughout His ministry on earth. He compared walking with Him to walking in the light instead of the darkness: "I am the light of the world. Anyone who follows Me will never walk in the darkness but will have the light of life … The light will be with you only a little longer. Walk while you have the light so that darkness doesn't overtake you. The one who walks in darkness doesn't know where he's going. While you have the light, believe in the light so that you may become sons of light" (John 8:12, 12:35–36).

My prayer for you is that you walk with the light of the world, Jesus, and that your prayers bring you into a growing intimacy with Him. He has made you perfect* and He loves you passionately, so humbly walk with Him in prayer.

Appendix

You Can Have Perfect* Intimacy with God

According to the Bible, what God is really after is a close, intimate relationship with each of us. He made us for that purpose, but through our own sin we sever the relationship. God will stop at nothing to restore it, however, because of His great love for us. By substituting His own perfect Son on the cross to pay the penalty for our sin, God brings reconciliation. Paul described it this way:

> Therefore if anyone is in Christ, there is a new creation; old things have passed away, and look, new things have come. Now everything is from God, who reconciled us to Himself through Christ and gave us the ministry of reconciliation: that is, in Christ, God was reconciling the world to Himself, not counting their trespasses against them, and He has committed the message of reconciliation to us. Therefore, we are ambassadors for Christ; certain that God is appealing through us, we

plead on Christ's behalf, "Be reconciled to God." (2 Corinthians 5:17–20)

It is up to each of us to choose how we will respond to God's appeal. He doesn't force it on you, but He continually offers His love, grace, mercy, and forgiveness through Jesus Christ.

How does all this work? We've already made plenty of mistakes, so even though we were made in God's image, that image is now marred. Does God remove the consequences of the mistakes you've made? Will He change history just for you? No, that doesn't happen. Just like the scar still visible from an old wound, you still live with the results of your decisions. The more mistakes you make, the more scars you have. The more severe your sins, the uglier the scars. Like any good parent, God allows you to experience the consequences of your actions.

Instead of correcting your errors, God chooses to make you perfect* by removing your guilt and punishment. Being perfect and holy, God requires justice. He cannot allow wrongdoing to go unpunished or He would violate His own integrity. His law is clear: those who violate it are guilty and deserve death. Paul said it this way: "There is no favoritism with God. All those who sinned without the law will also perish without the law, and all those who sinned under the law will be judged by the law ... For all have sinned and fall short of the glory of God" (Romans 2:11–12, 3:23).

None of us can stand before God in our own power. He already knew that, so He provided a Savior in the person of Jesus. Paul says of those who trust in Jesus, "They are justified freely by His grace through the redemption that is in Christ Jesus" (Romans 3:24), and "Therefore, no condemnation now exists for those in Christ Jesus" (Romans 8:1). What you could never do on your own, God has done for you.

The result is that God sees you as though you had never sinned: "As far as the east is from the west, so far has He removed our transgressions from us" (Psalm 103:12).

"I will place My law within them and write it on their hearts. I will be their God, and they will be My people … For I will forgive their wrongdoing and never again remember their sin" (Jeremiah 31:33–34).

How does one take God up on His offer? First, understand that it is your sin that has caused the problem by breaking your relationship with God. Take responsibility for that sin—acknowledge and confess it—and ask God to forgive you. If you are sincere He will readily forgive all your sin.

When you believe that Jesus is the Son of God and that He died on the cross to pay the penalty for your sin, God reconciles you to Himself as Paul described above.

Confirm to God and to yourself that you are taking those steps by simply going to Him in prayer and telling Him that you want to be reconciled to Him. Recognize that you are putting your faith in Jesus Christ to save you.

That's the beginning of life's most beautiful and bountiful union. Take joy in the fact that you have become a child of your heavenly Father! Not only are you now perfect*, but you can build intimacy with Him. And you can build intimacy with His other children through a local family of believers. Find a church that teaches God's word so that you have a support system as you grow into all that He desires.

Recommended Reading

Henry T. Blackaby and Claude V. King, *Experiencing God* (Nashville, Tennessee: Broadman & Holman, 1994). See especially Chapter 7, "God Pursues a Love Relationship with You."

Henry T. Blackaby and Richard Blackaby, *Hearing God's Voice* (Nashville, Tennessee: Broadman & Holman, 2002). Describes how God speaks to us with an unmistakable voice and how we can truly hear Him.

Gary D. Chapman, *The Love Languages of God* (Chicago, Illinois: Northfield Publishing, 2002). Dr. Chapman shows how our primary love language expresses itself in all aspects of our love relationship with God.

Gary D. Chapman, *Covenant Marriage* (Nashville, Tennessee: B&H Publishing Group, 2003). Demonstrates how love, communication, and intimacy are intertwined in true covenant marriage.

William A. Dembski, *The Design Revolution: Answering the Toughest Questions about Intelligent Design* (Downers Grove, Illinois: InterVarsity Press, 2004). Dembski shows how the latest scientific data points to the inescapable conclusion that the universe was created by an Intelligent Designer.

John Franklin and Chuck Lawless, *Spiritual Warfare* (Nashville, Tennessee: LifeWay Press, 2001). The authors expose the true biblical foundation for spiritual warfare in the life of the believer and the church.

Norman L. Geisler and Frank Turek, *I Don't Have Enough Faith to Be an Atheist* (Wheaton, Illinois: Crossway Books, 2004). The authors make a brilliant argument from the foundations of logic to prove that Christianity is true.

Max Lucado, *Just Like Jesus* (Nashville, Tennessee: Word Publishing, 1998). God loves you so much that He wants to change your heart to be the same as Jesus' heart.

Lee Strobel, *The Case for Christ* (Grand Rapids, Michigan: Zondervan,1998). In the first of a series, the author retraces his investigative steps from an avowed atheist to a committed follower of Jesus Christ.

CPSIA information can be obtained at www.ICGtesting.com
Printed in the USA
LVOW121329280613

340721LV00003B/51/P